SAMUEL ULLMAN AND "YOUTH"

Samuel Ullman and "Youth"

The Life,
the Legacy

MARGARET
ENGLAND
ARMBRESTER

With a Foreword by
Jiro M. Miyazawa

THE UNIVERSITY OF ALABAMA PRESS
Tuscaloosa and London

designed by zig zeigler

∞

The paper on which this book is printed
meets the minimum requirements of
American Standard for Information
Science-Permanence of Paper for
Printed Library Materials,
ANSI Z39.48-1984.

Library of Congress
Cataloging-in-Publication Data

Armbrester, Margaret E. (Margaret England), 1943–
    Samuel Ullman and "Youth" : the life, the legacy / by Margaret E.
Armbrester.
        p.   cm.
    Includes bibliographical references and index.
    ISBN 0-8173-0685-4 (alk. paper)
    1. Ullman, Samuel, 1840–1924.   Youth.   2. Ullman, Samuel,
1840–1924 — Biography.   3. Poets, American — 20th century —
Biography.   4. Businessmen — United States — Biography.
5. American poetry — Appreciation — Japan.   I. Title.
    PS3541.L4Z55   1993
    811'.52 — dc20   92-37414
                                                                CIP

British Library
Cataloguing-in-Publication Data available

YOUTH

Youth is not a time of life; it is a state of mind; it is not a matter of rosy cheeks, red lips and supple knees; it is a matter of the will, a quality of the imagination, a vigor of the emotions; it is the freshness of the deep springs of life.

Youth means a temperamental predominance of courage over timidity of the appetite, for adventure over the love of ease. This often exists in a man of sixty more than a boy of twenty. Nobody grows old merely by a number of years. We grow old by deserting our ideals.

Years may wrinkle the skin, but to give up enthusiasm wrinkles the soul. Worry, fear, self-distrust bows the heart and turns the spirit back to dust.

Whether sixty or sixteen, there is in every human being's heart the lure of wonder, the unfailing child-like appetite of what's next, and the joy of the game of living. In the center of your heart and my heart there is a wireless station; so long as it receives messages of beauty, hope, cheer, courage and power from men and from the Infinite, so long are you young.

When the aerials are down, and your spirit is covered with snows of cynicism and the ice of pessimism, then you are grown old, even at twenty, but as long as your aerials are up, to catch the waves of optimism, there is hope you may die young at eighty.

Contents

Foreword

Thousands of wonderful and sometimes strange fads have captured the public fancy in the almost five decades since the end of World War II. Most have been short-lived and soon faded away.

There is, however, a poem that has not only withstood the vicissitudes of time, but has spread around the world like the waves lapping at a beach. This is the poem "Youth," by Samuel Ullman.

In December 1945, the *Reader's Digest* published the poem and reported that General Douglas MacArthur, Commander of the Allied Forces, Far East, kept a copy of the poem near his desk.

Around that time, Yoshio Okada, a Japanese businessman, bought a copy of that December 1945 edition of the *Reader's Digest*, read the poem and was deeply affected by it. He translated it into Japanese and displayed it in his office as a guiding inspiration. Many of Okada's friends read the poem and were fascinated by its beauty. It began to receive national publicity through newspapers and magazines and became popular throughout Japan, especially among the intellectual community.

Part of the reason for this widespread popularity is the excellence of the translation. Yoshio Okada, a man of noble character, gifted with a profound philosophy of life and literary talent, translated the poem into a beautiful, soul-stirring Japanese version.

Samuel Ullman's "Youth" reflects the truth of life, and his outcry of spirituality touches the intrinsic nature of man.

I first encountered the poem in 1965 while busily engaged in the many responsibilities of establishing Toppan Moore Company, a joint venture business between Japan and Canada. It was given to me by a friend. I glanced at it and was immediately struck with its beauty and profound message. It was something worthy of sharing with others.

Over a span of some twenty years that I served as president of Toppan Moore, I distributed more than ten thousand copies of the poem.

In 1985, The Youth Association was formed in Tokyo. This is an organization of some 150 corporate members and 1800 individual members from all walks of life throughout Japan, from the island of Hokkaido in the north to Okinawa in the south. It has no political, religious or commercial association. It is simply an organization of people meeting to praise the spirit of youth, empathize with one another and share the joy and hope of life that is put forth so eloquently in Samuel Ullman's poem.

Japan has been completely rebuilt since the devastation of World War II. I believe Samuel Ullman's poem "Youth" played a part in this process by sustaining the Japanese mind with its inspiring message. Certainly, it is fair to say that the name of Samuel Ullman echoes throughout Japan, along with the name of his home state, Alabama.

I extend my deepest gratitude and respect to the memory of Samuel Ullman and wish The University of Alabama Press every success for this very worthy publication.

Jiro M. Miyazawa
Tokyo, Japan
May 1992

Acknowledgments

On a mild day in March 1989, my colleague and friend Dean Tennant McWilliams visited my office in the Ullman Building on the campus of the University of Alabama at Birmingham to ask if I would consider producing a brief biography on the late-nineteenth-century Birmingham civic leader for whom the building was named. He asked me to meet with local attorney Wyatt Haskell who represented a group within the local community that was interested in the life and work of Samuel Ullman. I met Haskell, who wondered aloud why a wide segment of the Japanese population knows of Ullman and Ullman's poem, "Youth," while most Alabamians and Americans have heard of neither. To me, that seemed a reasonable question, so I agreed to do some preliminary research to see if I wanted to pursue writing a brief overview of Ullman's life. I soon found that Ullman's life incorporated what I like best about history: It was a good story.

Two years later, I completed a larger manuscript than originally envisioned. In that time I came to know, appreciate, respect, and have deep affection for Mayer Ullman Newfield, who generously, energetically, and with unwavering optimism aided and abetted my research. This grandson of Samuel Ullman opened his heart, memory, and files to me during the course of this project. In Natchez, Mississippi, his cousin Elaine Lehman and her husband Robert were equally hospitable and helpful as I researched the Natchez part of Ullman's life. Another Ullman in-law, Hank Gaggstatter of Miami,

Florida, became an enthusiastic supporter of the project and came forward with interesting and useful documents related to Ullman's life and career.

As all researchers must, I depended during this project on the help, knowledge, and pleasant dispositions of librarians and archivists across the country. My friends at the Archives and the Tutwiler Collection of the Birmingham Public Library — Yvonne Crumpler, Jim Murray, Don Veasey, Marvin Whiting — were, as always, full of information and unfailingly cheerful when they saw me approach. Of the many librarians and archivists to whom I am indebted in research facilities in Louisville, Norfolk, Washington, Cincinnati, and Natchez, one stands out in my memory: Connie Randazzo, who directs the Natchez-Adams (County) School District Library–Media Services, spent several days locating and searching the earliest records of the Natchez Board of Visitors, the city's early board of education. She combed those records for references to Ullman, and when she discovered the "mother lode" her excitement and delight matched mine. Historical detective work is fun, but it becomes especially sweet when someone else joins you in the discovery process.

Colleagues in the UAB Department of History, especially Virginia Hamilton, buoyed my spirit by giving encouragement and acting as critical readers of the manuscript. Katharine Stark, Jodie Hudson, and Janene Riley remained patient when both the computer and I tried to self-destruct. James Penick and Debra Givens provided me with every support and consideration to facilitate completion of this work. Finally, my family — Rodger, Amy, and Rod — showed their usual forebearance with my always having my nose in a book or a stack of papers. Their reward, I hope, is that by studying Ullman's life I have grown younger in spirit. While my debt of gratitude is great, I alone bear responsibility for the content of this book.

SAMUEL ULLMAN AND "YOUTH"

CHAPTER 1

"Youth": A Philosophy, a Bridge

In late June 1990, Kokichi Hagiwara, the majority owner and new chairman of National Steel Corporation, stood before a press gathering in Pittsburgh, Pennsylvania and pulled from his briefcase a single sheet of paper that held, he explained, his plan for making National Steel a more profitable business. The paper contained no tables, graphs, or profit-and-loss statements. To the surprise of those present, it was merely a brief prose poem entitled "Youth," written around the turn of the century by Samuel Ullman of Birmingham, Alabama. The poem, said Hagiwara, "touched me at the core of my heart," and embodied his philosophy for creating a successful future for National Steel.[1]

Ullman's poem, "Youth," has appeared in "Dear Abby" and "Ann Landers" columns and in *Reader's Digest*. United States senators and a television anchorwoman have quoted from it. Anthologies of Ullman's poetry have sold widely in Japan. Yet the poet and his poetry remain largely unknown in America. Soldier, merchant, rabbi, philosopher, and progressive community activist, Ullman lived an authentic American life — a life that stretched from Europe to America and, through his poetry, to Japan.

In 1944, twenty years after Ullman's death and during the waning months of World War II, war correspondent Colonel Frederick Palmer visited General Douglas MacArthur at his Manila headquarters. Palmer's attention was drawn to an arrangement on the wall behind MacArthur's desk where pictures of presidents George Washington and Abraham

Samuel Ullman, April 13, 1840–March 21, 1924. Relatives, noting the thinning of Ullman's face and neck, believe that this may be one of the last photographs taken of him. Although known as an exuberantly happy man, Ullman often posed with a somewhat stern expression on his face. (Photograph courtesy Mayer U. Newfield.)

Lincoln hung and, between them, a framed document entitled "How to Stay Young." Palmer inquired about the poetic essay and the general told him that he received the unattributed work from an admirer, John W. Lewis, Jr., in April 1942 while he (MacArthur) was stationed in Melbourne, Australia. When Colonel Palmer wrote of this exchange and reproduced the poem in the September 30, 1945 *This Week* magazine supplement to thousands of newspapers around the country, the demand for copies was enormous.[2]

Determined to see their ancestor recognized as the author of the poem, members of Ullman's family sent *This Week* a full, original version of "Youth" as it appeared in the 1922 edition of *From the Summit of Years, Four Score*, an anthology of Ullman's poetry published by family members after the celebration of his eightieth birthday. Ullman was acknowledged as the author of the poem when *Reader's Digest* reproduced the *This Week* article in its December 1945 issue. The poem also appeared in a Japanese version of *Reader's Digest* in January 1946. Japanese soldiers in the process of repatriation from Pacific locations read this edition while on ships returning them home. Slowly "Youth" began to invade the Japanese consciousness.[3]

This "invasion" was encouraged by the respect which a subject Japanese people held for MacArthur, who hung Ullman's poem in the same decorative arrangement on the wall of his office in Tokyo when he arrived there in September 1945 to oversee occupied Japan. Among the most important of the Japanese leaders who came to that office to consult with MacArthur on matters related to their recovery was the eminent businessman Yasuzaemon Matsunaga, who later earned the title "King of Electric Power" (Den-Ryo-Ku-O). Matsunaga took note of the poem hanging on the general's wall, translated it into Japanese, and distributed it to friends and associates. Matsunaga's fame, as well as that of Mac-

Arthur, helped to spread the work's reputation among a small but elite group of businessmen and intellectuals in Japan.[4]

As "Youth" made its way into Japan's culture, it remained almost unknown in the United States. The poetic essay, with Ullman cited as author, appeared in a 1934 anthology, *The Silver Treasury*, compiled by Jane Manners (New York: Samuel French), and the privately published collection of Ullman's poems, *From the Summit of Years, Four Score*, was cited in Joseph L. Baron's *Treasury of Jewish Quotations* (New York: Crown, 1956). In 1952, *The Monitor*, a publication of the Associated Industries of New York State, sought MacArthur's permission to use the "creed" in a future issue. Lawrence Bunker, MacArthur's aide, responded by citing Ullman's authorship but continued, "General MacArthur has, of course, no objection to your reference to him in the caption."[5]

After his "retirement" from the Korean conflict in 1952, MacArthur returned to the United States for the first time in sixteen years and became a corporate advisor and much sought-after speaker. On January 26, 1955, his seventy-fifth birthday, MacArthur gave three well-publicized speeches in Los Angeles, California. During the evening event, before an audience of American Legionnaires at the Ambassador Hotel, MacArthur delivered a talk later described as "one of his best in delivery and effectiveness." According to MacArthur's biographer, the portion of the speech that received the most notice and comment was a quotation MacArthur used from a "little-known, brief essay that some thought he penned but that was actually composed by a long deceased Southern business and civic leader, Samuel Ullman." In that speech MacArthur declared that he was still young at seventy-five because he believed that "youth is not entirely a time of life — it is a state of mind." Previously, in 1952, MacArthur had quoted from Ullman's poem in a speech before a Remington Rand executives' dinner, but the 1955 speech was more widely covered by major newspapers and magazines, most of which included portions of Ullman's work in their coverage of the speech.[6]

One journalist who was impressed with the message of the quotation used by MacArthur sought the identity of its author. George Sokolsky wrote an article for the New York *Journal American* in which he identified Ullman as the author of the original essay. Later, during MacArthur's final illness in 1964, news articles again carried portions of "Youth" to explain the general's philosophy of life and his determined will to live.[7]

The publicity surrounding MacArthur's seventy-fifth birthday and his death no doubt revived interest in Ullman's poetic essay both in Japan and the United States. Yet Ullman's authorship continued to be largely unheralded. Unattributed portions of "Youth" appeared in Allen Saunders's "Mary Worth" cartoon strip on January 1, 1971, in the "Ann Landers" column of February 15, 1977, and in "Dear Abby" on June 25, 1982. On June 8, 1968, Senator Edward M. Kennedy quoted from the poem in his eulogy at the funeral of his slain brother Robert, who earlier had used the same portion in a speech before an audience of South African young people. "The answer [to the world's problems]," said Senator Kennedy quoting his brother, "is to rely on youth, not a time of life but a state of mind, a temper of the will, a quality of imagination, a predominance of courage over timidity, of the appetite for adventure over the love of ease." During a November 1991 story that aired on the "Sunday Today" program, NBC news anchorwoman Mary Alice Williams quoted lines from "Youth" and credited nineteenth-century English poet William Wordsworth as its author. From the 1960s through the early 1990s, "Youth" received limited recognition in the United States, but Ullman's authorship did not.[8]

During the 1960s, meanwhile, Ullman's poem began by various means to capture the attention and affection of a larger audience in Japan, especially among businessmen.

Kounosuke Matsushita, creator of the Matsushita Group, reminisced when he was ninety-two years of age (in 1987) that when he was seventy he felt too old to pursue a major expansion of his business. In the mid-1960s, as he began to establish the Panasonic division of the Matsushita Group, the founder feared that this new venture might be too demanding for the fading mental and physical energies of a man of his age. Then he discovered a copy of "Youth." Matsushita memorized portions of the poem and, for inspiration and encouragement, often repeated its lines to himself and to others. In the words of the poem he found a renewed enthusiasm and energy to continue building his business. He copied a portion of the poem in his own calligraphy and sent reproduced copies to each of his more than 20,000 dealers around the world. Referred to at his death at the age of ninety-four as "one of Japan's leading postwar industrialists," billionaire Matsushita regularly greeted people with, "Have you made some money?" Yet this pragmatist found in the simple message of "Youth" spiritual and mental refreshment.[9]

Another successful Japanese businessman, Kyoichi Itoh, received a copy of the poem from his father, Chubei Itoh, founder of the internationally known trading firm C. Itoh and Company. The elder Itoh had received the poem from Matsunaga and both he and his son, who became a noted entrepreneur in his own right, used portions of it in speeches they made at social and business functions. Osamu Uno succeeded Kyoichi Itoh as Chairman of Toyo Boseki (the largest textile manufacturer in Japan) and later became chairman of the Kansai Federation of Economic Organizations (Kan-Kei-Ren). Uno came to know and appreciate "Youth" in 1965, during the publicity surrounding MacArthur's death. He, too, began to use the poem in speeches, and in 1982 he quoted from "Youth" in two articles he wrote for a leading economic journal, *The Japan Economic Journal* (*Nihon Keizai Shimbun*), the Japanese equivalent of *The Wall Street Journal*. The response to the articles and requests for copies of the poem astonished him. One of those who contacted Uno regarding the poem was Munehisa "Sam" Sakuyama. He and Uno became friends and developed a business association centered on their common interest in "Youth" and its author, Ullman. Uno and Sakuyama explained the poem's popularity by suggesting that, after World War II, Japanese citizens worked under "great tension and pressure in [a] controlled society." Under such stress, Japanese businessmen yearned for more satisfaction and meaning in their lives. "Youth" encouraged individual responsibility, "which is not unique to Americans," and offered the hope that people could stay young and strong by thinking optimistically.[10]

Sakuyama visited Birmingham in 1983 to learn more about the person he had begun to call the "Phantom Poet" who wrote the simple, optimistic, and influential work that gained the affection of so many Japanese citizens. In Birmingham, Sakuyama met Ullman's grandson, Mayer Ullman Newfield, who told him of Ullman's community services, shared additional writings of Ullman with him, and escorted him to the home where Ullman lived until his death and to the building that bears Ullman's name on the campus of the University of Alabama at Birmingham. Thirty-eight years after the Japanese discovered "Youth," they were finally beginning to discover its author. Armed with the additional writings of Ullman, Sakuyama and Uno collaborated in translating and publishing in Japanese *The Poem Titled "Youth": The Phantom Poet, Samuel Ullman (Seishun-to-Iunano-shi).* This book includes a brief biographical sketch of Ullman's life, several versions of "Youth," information on how the Japanese came to know "Youth," and letters written by and about Ullman. As the Japanese learned more about Ullman and especially about his devotion to Judaism and American individualism, "Youth" took on even greater meaning.[11]

Jiro M. Miyazawa also came to know and appreciate

"Youth" in 1965, when he was fifty-six years old and busily involved in establishing Toppan Moore Company, a business-form printing company jointly operated by Japan's Toppan Printing and Canada's Moore Corporation. Over a span of twenty years, Miyazawa distributed more than ten thousand copies of the poem to friends and business associates. He was amazed at the thousands of appreciative responses he received, and that overwhelming reaction led him, in 1985, to help create The Youth Association in Tokyo. By 1992, this organization enjoyed a membership of over 1800 individual and 150 corporate members. Members study "Youth" and the writings of older philosophers and are dedicated to creating a "youthful and richly creative society."[12]

Uno and Sakuyama's book, *The Poem Titled "Youth,"* sold well, but its sales increased dramatically after a widely publicized celebration was held in 1987 in Tokyo to honor "Youth" and its author. The celebration occurred after a business meeting brought together Tatsuro Ishida, chairman of the Fuji Television Network and a pioneer in the use of audio and video cassettes, and Jonas Rosenfield, president of the American Film Marketing Association and another of Ullman's grandsons. The two men met in early 1987 to discuss ways to discourage the piracy of taped materials. As their discussions ended, Rosenfield casually mentioned that he hoped, while he was in Japan, to find someone familiar with his grandfather's poem, "Youth." Ishida could hardly believe his ears. With great excitement he pulled from his pocket a creased copy of the poem that he carried at all times and began to ask Rosenfield about his grandfather's life. As Ishida told friends of his fortuitous meeting with Rosenfield, plans for a celebration began to take shape. Ishida, Uno, Sakuyama, and others hosted the party, held in Tokyo on September 22, 1987. The gathering brought together Ullman's grandsons, Newfield and Rosenfield, the governor of Tokyo, and three hundred influential Japanese political and business people.[13]

During the evening, numerous guests offered explanations

for the great affection "Youth" enjoys among the Japanese. Matsushita's grandson read a message from his ailing grandfather in which the elder Matsushita admitted, "Ullman's poem fills my thoughts." Jiro Miyazawa, also a host of the celebration, said, "Its message is to live young, live strong, live a life of work." Ishida explained that "Youth" is to the Japanese what spinach is to Popeye, a source of vitality. Ishida also suggested that Japanese businessmen, having achieved success and affluence, are now searching for spiritual meaning. "Youth" contains a message of how to live beautifully, offered Uno. The party was videotaped and shown later on Japanese television. As part of the event's entertainment a song based on "Youth" ("Seishun") was composed, performed, and recorded for distribution by a popular Japanese group, The Alfee.[14]

After that event, Sakuyama and Uno published a Japanese version of *From the Summit of Years, Four Score*, the collection of Ullman's poetry published in 1922 by his family as a permanent commemoration of his life. This Japanese edition is now in its second printing, and profits from this book and the earlier work on Ullman are donated to a scholarship fund in Ullman's name at the University of Alabama at Birmingham. Audio and video cassette tapes of Ullman's life and work also have been created and disseminated in Japan.[15]

The poem, while best known and appreciated among the business leaders of Japan, has a message that is applicable and inspiring to a broad audience. This was demonstrated by Chiyohiko Asano, a retired radio and television executive who used the poem in his talks to young men incarcerated in Japanese reformatories. He asked the young listeners to comment on his lectures, and many of them embraced the message of "Youth." They told Asano that, despite the wasted early years of their lives, Ullman's message gave them hope that the remainder of their lives could be lived usefully and with the vigor of youth.[16]

The message of "Youth" continues to provide many Japanese with encouragement and renewed energies as they and their nation enjoy maturity and success after the wartime period of failure and defeat. The message of "Youth" requires individual responsibility for the direction of one's life. It makes no excuses for failures, demonstrates no nostalgia for past glories, and provides no corporate guilt to minimize personal accountability. The substance of "Youth" came naturally from the simple ebb and flow of its author's eighty-four year life — a life of purpose, service, and optimism. It is not surprising that readers find inspiration in it.

CHAPTER 2

Old World, New World

Because they were Jews, Samuel Ullman's parents, Jacob Ullman and Lena Goldsmith Ullman, were forced to wait two years before finally being allowed to marry on June 19, 1839 in Hechingen, Germany.[1] Jacob, thirty-four, and Lena, thirty-two, had grown accustomed by that time to the restrictions placed on Jews by the repressive Germanic Confederation government. The Congress of Vienna created this organization of thirty-eight German states in 1814 ostensibly to guarantee continued peace after the long unrest of the Napoleonic era. In reality, the Confederation was an attempt to destroy the movement toward liberal reforms that had begun in Germany. Government officials reestablished Jewish ghettos, limited the number of Jewish marriages, and forced Jews into menial and disagreeable jobs by limiting their numbers in certain professions. The Confederation government squelched the liberal movements begun during the revolutionary and Napoleonic eras, limited public meetings, introduced strict censorship of publications, and spied on the political activities of individuals and universities.[2]

Jacob Ullman, a liberal Jew who favored expanded suffrage rights and guarantees of liberties, wanted a safer and more secure future for his wife and their infant son born April 13, 1840. They chose their first child's name carefully because in Jewish tradition the name given a child was believed to shape or reveal his future character or deeds. Samuel Ullman was named for his grandfather, Rabbi Samuel ben Isaac Ullman. In 1841 the Ullmans moved with their son to the Alsace region of France where they anticipated possessing more fully the rights enjoyed by others.[3]

In France four more children were born to Jacob and Lena between 1842 and 1847. Then in 1848 democratic revolutions throughout Europe again broke out. In France tensions arose in response to King Louis Philippe's unwillingness to allow most of the French population a voice in the political process and his ineffectiveness in dealing with food shortages and problems caused by industrialization. The Ullmans felt the violence of these times in an intimate and terrifying way when their six-year-old son, Edward, was caught in cross fire and shot, although not seriously wounded. The revolutions failed to accomplish reforms and President Louis-Napoleon (later emperor) began to increase his power dramatically, taking steps to continue in power indefinitely. Jacob, troubled by these events and fearing a renewed loss of privileges, gathered his family and in late 1850 sailed for America.[4]

The Ullmans became part of a massive movement of immigrants who fled the disruptions of Europe in the mid-nineteenth century to pursue opportunity and tolerance in the United States. Between 1849 and 1880, approximately 250,000 European Jews, most of them "liberal democrats" (as Samuel Ullman described his father), arrived in the United States. Following a trip that took fifty-six days, the Ullmans debarked in New Orleans on January 17, 1851 only to spend several more days aboard another boat traveling up the Mississippi River to Port Gibson, Mississippi, where Jacob's brother, Isaac, had settled earlier.[5]

A local merchant described Port Gibson at mid-century as a "fine little country town, eight miles from the Mississippi, whither a bayou leads that carries flatboats up to the town." Although it was smaller than Natchez, Vicksburg, or Jackson, Port Gibson figured significantly in the social and cultural life of the "hinterland" and was regularly mentioned as a serious choice for the location of the state capital in debates between

1822 and 1832. By 1860 Port Gibson boasted a rail line and a Presbyterian college, neither of which Natchez enjoyed.[6]

Although the foreign-born population of Mississippi was minuscule, the 1860 census revealed that approximately half of those involved in trade and commerce in Port Gibson were, like Jacob Ullman, European immigrants. Jews in Mississippi in 1860 numbered no more than six hundred, but there were enough besides Samuel and his father living in Port Gibson by 1859 to form a congregation calling itself Gemiluth Chassed. Yet neither this congregation nor any other in Mississippi had built a synagogue as late as 1861. Jewish immigrants like the Ullmans met little discrimination in the South and, in fact, discovered among their Protestant neighbors an appreciation for them as "people of the Book." Their minority status and religion set them apart, especially on Sundays, but most Jews in the late-nineteenth-century South assimilated comfortably into the economic and civic life of their adopted communities.[7]

The Ullmans found this to be true as they made their home in Port Gibson where Jacob joined his brother Isaac in managing a butchering business. Isaac Ullman and his wife, Agatha, died in 1853 during an epidemic of yellow fever. Jacob and Lena adopted their two children, Pauline, six, and Simon, two, who joined Samuel, thirteen, Berthe, nine, Matilda, six, and Marcus, four, in the Ullman household. (Samuel's sister, Dorothea, died in infancy in 1846, and Edward, having survived the revolutions in France, died at the age of ten soon after the family arrived in Port Gibson.)[8]

At thirteen, Samuel took Uncle Isaac's place in the butcher shop and, as he put it, began to act "the part of a man." After making the shop's daily meat deliveries, he went immediately to school where fellow students teased him because he smelled of beef. The family business prospered, and Jacob expanded his shop into a small grocery and purchased two slaves. By the time Samuel was fifteen years old, his work had enlarged to include buying cattle from local planters for slaughtering in his father's shop. As useful as Samuel was to his business, Jacob must have become concerned that his eldest child was not receiving adequate instruction in traditional Judaism. In 1856 Jacob sent Samuel, then sixteen years old, to school in Louisville, Kentucky.[9]

Another, older man of the name Samuel Ullman was among those who incorporated the Adas (Adath) Israel congregation in Louisville, Kentucky in 1843. This Samuel Ullman, like each of the other thirty-three incorporators of the first Jewish congregation in Louisville, was a relative newcomer to the city. He was the proprietor of S. Ullman and Company, a popular wholesale and retail dry goods store located at 432 West Main. Ullman served on the board of directors of Adas Israel when the congregation in 1847 began raising funds to build a temple. By 1848 construction on a facility began at Fourth between Green (now Liberty) and Walnut, and the congregation decided to establish a school to educate its children in primarily, but not exclusively, religious studies. In September 1849, the congregation hired Bernard H. Gotthelf of Philadelphia as "Chasan, Teacher and Lecturer" at a salary of $1,200 a year, from which he was expected to pay not only his own expenses but also the expenses of those who assisted him in teaching the "Hebrew, English, German, religion and elementary studies" that comprised the academic curricula of the School. Gotthelf was promoted to rabbi of the congregation in 1851 and served in that position until 1866.[10]

While no certain link has been found between the younger Samuel Ullman of Port Gibson, Mississippi and the older Samuel Ullman of Louisville, Kentucky, no doubt Jacob sent his son to board with a Kentucky relative of the same name so that he could attend the Jewish congregational school. It may have been young Samuel's association with the Louisville Ullman that sparked his developing interest in marketing dry goods, and certainly the Louisville experience must have helped to develop a lifelong interest in and devotion to education. It is also likely that Samuel's studies with Rabbi Gotthelf played a significant role in inspiring Ullman's devotion to Judaism, a commitment that marked his life and career. In short, although few details can be found about the eighteen months Ullman spent in Louisville, the period was significant enough that, at the age of eighty, he remembered it in a brief biographical essay he wrote to a nephew.[11]

Ullman's formal education ended in 1858 when he returned to Port Gibson and became, as he put it, the "first assistant" in his father's growing business. His father taught him what the schoolroom could not—the virtue of work, the necessity of perseverance, and the value of family, democracy, liberty, and tolerance. Ullman's life suggests that he was a quick and willing learner. Indeed, he so impressed two "big-hearted" planters from the Port Gibson community that they inexplicably offered to pay his way through college. Concerned that his father's business might fail to prosper without his services, he declined their generous offer. Later in his life, a life he devoted to self-education and to improving the educational opportunities of others, Ullman drolly recalled that he came to be called "Doctor" Ullman. "I must have gotten the degree in the butcher shop or cowpen," he joked.[12]

Ullman's secure life in Port Gibson ended with Mississippi's secession from the Union on January 9, 1861. Although he took little part in presecession debates or activities, Ullman was elected secretary of the Breckinridge and Lane Club of Claiborne County, Mississippi. These clubs arose throughout the South in 1860 to support the candidates for president and vice president on the Southern Democrat ticket in 1860.[13] That ticket failed to carry the day, and the South's response to Lincoln's election and his determination to preserve the Union led to open warfare at Fort Sumter in April 1861.

On May 31, 1861, Ullman, twenty-one years of age and a resident of the United States for only nine years, enrolled as a private for an initial period of twelve months in the Mississippi militia company of Captain John Taylor Moore. A month later several Mississippi companies including Moore's were reorganized into Company G, also known as the Fairview Rifles or Claiborne Rifles, of the Sixteenth Mississippi Regiment. By whatever name, Ullman and the other members of Company G were now members of the Confederate army.[14]

Private Samuel Ullman enlisted and fought, as most Southerners initially believed they did, in defense of his homeland and for lofty constitutional principles. He became one of nine hundred men in the Sixteenth Regiment under Captain Carnot Posey's command. Posey, who apprenticed in Jefferson Davis's regiment during the Mexican-American War, led his men to action in northern Virginia in late July 1861. The August 31, 1861 muster roll of the Sixteenth Regiment reported Private Ullman "Detached for Regimental Band," playing an unspecified instrument. He held musician status on the muster rolls through December 1861.[15]

The days between summer 1861 and spring 1862 were generally quiet ones for Ullman and Company G as George B. McClellan, the new general-in-chief of the Union Army of the Potomac, delayed and dawdled. Ullman rarely reminisced about his wartime experiences, but one event of that time was fixed in his memory. He told his grandson that during that quiet period in the winter of 1862 his father Jacob traveled to Virginia to visit him. As Ullman moved to greet his father, the elder Ullman burst into tears at the sight of blood on the snow coming from the torn feet of his son, whose worn boots no longer offered any protection. Perhaps that is why, once the fighting began, Ullman crept onto the battleground one night and removed a pair of boots from the feet of a dead Yankee soldier. Upon his return to camp, he discovered a packet of letters from the slain soldier's sweetheart hidden in the boots. After the war, Ullman returned the letters to the woman, and the two briefly corresponded.[16]

In May 1862 the quiet and waiting ended when the Sixteenth Mississippi Regiment was assigned to General Thomas J. ("Stonewall") Jackson's command, the only Mississippi company to serve in Jackson's army. They joined General Jackson in the Valley Campaign which ended June 9, 1862 with Jackson's 17,000 men defeating Union forces numbering 33,000. Ullman was wounded in the June 8 Cross Keys engagement of the Valley Campaign, but was able to participate in the Seven Days' battles that quickly followed. Jackson's forces had moved toward Richmond to join Robert E. Lee who had been appointed general of the Army of Northern Virginia on June 1, 1862. For seven days McClellan's forces repulsed all Confederate attacks and inflicted heavy losses on the southern troops. Yet when the Seven Days' battles ended on July 1, the Union army had been expelled from the outskirts of Richmond, and the campaign resulted in a strategic Confederate victory. Ullman's only recorded reaction to the carnage he observed during those battle-filled days was to write that he was wounded at Cross Keys, an injury of unspecified nature, and had "participated" in the Seven Days' Battle.[17]

In August 1862 Ullman was again with Jackson and Lee in the Confederate defeat of Union forces at Second Bull Run. Then with little break, Lee's forces invaded Maryland where, on September 17, 1862, forty thousand Confederate troops were caught by McClellan's superior forces near Sharpsburg, Maryland for what became the bloodiest one-day battle of the war. The Battle of Antietam ended in a draw militarily, but losses were monstrous: Union dead, 2,108; Union wounded, 9,549; Confederate dead, 2,700; Confederate wounded, 9,029.[18] The losses of the Sixteenth Regiment were equally dramatic: Of the 228 who went into battle, 144 were killed or wounded, including Ullman, who received permanent damage to the hearing in his left ear when a shell exploded near him. Having suffered two injuries in the service of the Confederacy, with his company decimated, and needed by his family at home, Ullman furnished a substitute and was discharged from the Confederate army on November 7, 1862.[19]

Just short of six feet tall, lean and erect, broad browed and square jawed, with brown hair and bright blue eyes, and with his hearing impaired permanently due to service in the Confederacy, Ullman hoped for a safer and brighter future. His family and ethnic heritage, his religion, his education, work and wartime experiences had shaped him to that point. He returned to Port Gibson a more mature man, physically and emotionally ready to meet the future. He rarely spoke of his Confederate experiences and never attended the popular reunions of soldiers that were held regularly. And once their freedom was won, emancipated slaves had no better friend in the South than former Confederate Private Samuel Ullman.[20] Why would an oppressed, immigrant Jew like Ullman become a defender of the Confederacy? Observers of life in Mississippi offer the explanation that southern Jews were, like their neighbors, products of their surroundings who viewed themselves first and foremost as southerners. "After all he [a southern Jew] could not escape his environment."[21]

CHAPTER 3

I Am Hebrew

Ullman recuperated and worked in Port Gibson until the war ended. Finding opportunities in the postwar city too limited, and hopeful of renewing friendships with the men from Natchez with whom he had served in the Sixteenth Mississippi Regiment, Ullman moved to Natchez in July 1865. That city and its beautiful homes had escaped the worst ravages of the Civil War when it surrendered without a fight to General Benjamin F. Butler's troops in April 1862. In fact, immediately after the war Natchez was in better shape than much of the South. Given Natchez's prime location on the Mississippi River, its townspeople had every expectation that the economy and business of the city would recover fully. Ullman anticipated profiting as well. The city's hopes seemed to be fulfilled when the 1880 census reported that the population of Adams County had increased during the preceding decade from 19,084 to 22,649. But Natchez, like most of the South, found postwar recovery difficult — indeed, ultimately impossible — to sustain.[1]

Upon arriving in Natchez, Ullman associated himself with the Hebra Kadusha, a small, loosely organized Orthodox Jewish association that held regular meetings in a fire station. Always an impatient man, Ullman soon joined others in the group who, preferring Reform ways, grew weary of the Orthodox, European order of service, the rare attendance of women and children, and the lack of any plan for building a temple. In the winter of 1865 this group of progressive thinkers organized a congregation that called itself B'nai

Israel.[2] B'nai Israel reflected the Reform movement in Judaism, a movement that arose in the early 1800s in Germany but grew most quickly in the United States. To many Orthodox Jews, Reform Jews seemed too modern, daring, revolutionary, and rational. Reform Jews, perhaps desiring to be more "American" and more like their new Protestant neighbors, favored shorter, simpler, vernacular worship, sermons, and hymns. They emphasized a liberal, social teaching: good works and social improvement, the ethical more than the ritual side of religion, the brotherhood of man, and the inclusion of programs for women and children. The practice of a simpler and more secular religion helped Reform Jews to appear less foreign or strange in their American communities.[3]

Nothing marked Ullman's life and character as much as his brand of Judaism which, he wrote, "helped me, like my father, to become a democrat," a "full-sized American." In a lecture delivered in 1876, Ullman described the essence of Judaism as a belief in an infinite, loving, merciful God; in the immortality of the soul; and in the universality of love, justice, and liberty — characteristics that Jews had a "holy mission as a race" to spread throughout their societies. He declared his belief that the simplicity and purity of Judaic belief made it compatible with the constant progress of society and science, an assertion that predates by almost a decade a similar position in the "Pittsburgh Platform" approved by Reform Jews in 1885. In a ringing affirmation of his Judaism, he wrote:

> This is Judaism, my friends. This is our religion. Need we be ashamed of it? Shall we be afraid of professing it, of acknowledging that we are proud of being Jews? Look around you. Compare and investigate and you will not discover any religion more simple or elevating. This is our pride, our joy and glory. Away then with all cowardice. Away with indifference. Away with all pusilamity [sic]. Let us like our fathers remain true and firm and then when we are asked, What is your occupation? Whence came you? What is your

country? Of what people are you, we can proudly answer as Jonah of old, *Ivri Onochi* — I am Hebrew.[4]

The B'nai Israel congregation quickly recognized Ullman's leadership ability. He became a lay reader and organized a Sunday school for children. Not unlike Protestants, European Jews in America adopted Sunday school programs as a way to continue to teach children the traditions of their faith. Ullman agreed with a general feeling within the Natchez congregation that the Jewish children of the city were "growing up like heathen[s]" for lack of religious instruction. Believing strongly that the involvement and energies of the women of the congregation were necessary to the success of B'nai Israel and its Sunday school, Ullman engaged the services of Emma Mayer to assist him in running the Sunday school program.[5]

Emma, the daughter of John and Jannette Reis Mayer, moved with them in 1841 from New Orleans to Natchez. Emma's parents had met on the boat that brought them to the United States, and in 1835 John Mayer married seventeen-year-old Jannette in New Orleans. Emma was born two years later on July 9, 1837, the first of fourteen children born into the family. The Mayers established themselves as an important and influential family in the Jewish community and economic life of Natchez. Mayer opened a "fashionable" shoe store in the city, helped to organize the original Jewish congregation in 1861, and served as that congregation's president until the Civil War "paralyzed Jewish activities in Natchez as it did everywhere else." During the war Emma, her mother, and her sister carried contraband through Union lines to Confederate soldiers by suspending shirts, boots, and medicines under their hoop skirts.[6]

Emma survived those wartime exploits and joined Ullman as co-worker in the Sunday school program, and Ullman always credited her with its success. Working as a team, they soon fell in love and became engaged. In announcing Emma's engagement, mother-in-law-to-be Jannette wrote to friends with somewhat lukewarm enthusiasm that "the man is not rich, but has a nice business and is well-spoken of." She also described Ullman's parents, who still resided in Port Gibson, as "nice old people" who were pleased with their son's choice of a bride.[7] The local newspaper announced Samuel and Emma's marriage, which took place at the Mayer residence in Natchez on Tuesday, May 24, 1867.[8] The affection between twenty-seven-year-old Samuel and Emma, who was almost thirty, was ardent. He loved her unreservedly and also came to have deep affection and respect for his new family, especially for his mother-in-law. He remembered Mrs. Mayer many years later as always being busy with "relieving distress, nursing sick through epidemics of yellow fever, regardless of color or race." By these actions, Ullman wrote, she brought "home the best concepts of Religion."[9] He and Emma followed her example in devoting themselves to similar good deeds

The business to which Mrs. Mayer alluded in her letter to friends was the Ullman and Laub Mercantile. From that store, located at the corner of Franklin and Commerce streets, Ullman and his cousin David Laub sold dry goods, groceries, and plantation supplies to both local and outlying citizens.[10] R. G. Dun Records (now Dun and Bradstreet) chronicles the unsteady and sometimes shaky course of the business. In January 1867 Ullman and Laub was reported to have a good business capacity, but by June 1868 the records recorded Ullman as a silent partner with a notation that the proprietors "don't stand well." The February 1869 report advised against extending much credit to the firm, and in July 1869 there was a notation that "'U' stands well, 'L' does not" in reputation. By July 1870 business improved and the company stood "very well and [was] making money." The business gave prompt and energetic service, according to the January 1872 report. The

Ullman and Laub Mercantile in Natchez, Mississippi, circa 1880. Ullman
owned and operated this business with his cousin, David Laub. (Photograph
courtesy of Mrs. Robert [Elaine] Lehman.)

June 1874 report described the company as behind in payments, but by October of that year Ullman and Laub were paying their debts in a timely fashion. The Dun service warned nonetheless of a "close record this fall and winter." The March 1875 report stated that the business was doing a "safe but small business," and also disclosed that "L owns a residence. U owns no real estate." Between 1876 and 1878 Ullman and Laub Mercantile enjoyed good prospects, held the confidence of the community, enjoyed good credit, and paid its debts well. In a biographical sketch of June 18, 1879, the report described Ullman as a married man, forty years of age, whose character ("char"), habits ("habs"), prospects ("pros"), credit, and standing ("stdg") in the community were good. The last report prepared for Ullman and Laub Mercantile by R. G. Dun continued to report good prospects for the business.[11]

After July 1879 Ullman and Laub disappeared from those records without explanation. Natchez city records reveal a payment of twenty dollars to Ullman and Laub Mercantile for blankets it furnished the city in 1871 for use with the indigent sick. Ullman and Laub also participated in a local controversy when their names appeared in a newspaper article that included a lengthy list of taxpayers who refused to pay city taxes in 1872. The resistance would continue, these angry taxpayers warned, until the city amended the existing revenue ordinance so that it conformed with the city's charter that limited city tax rates on real or personal property to two percent. These Natchez revolutionaries argued in the best American tradition that only a limited tax rate could "safeguard against unlimited oppression in the matter of municipal taxation."[12]

Although his business went through uneasy periods, Ullman's family life flourished in Natchez. Samuel and Emma's happy marriage and lasting affection found expression not only in the poems that Ullman wrote about Emma, but also in the eight children they had, six of whom lived to maturity. The children came with regularity: Edward Goldsmith (born 1869), Sidney Mayer (1871), Isaac Wise (1873), Leah (1874), Moses Montefiore (1875), Henry Goldsmith (1877), Elenora (1879), and Caroline Frank (1880).[13]

Emma and Samuel shared not only growing family responsibilities, but also an enthusiastic and energetic penchant for community and religious service. In August 1867, members of Temple B'nai Israel in Natchez elected Ullman president of the congregation, an event observers said "opened a new chapter in the life of the congregation." His "official" involvement with the congregation appeared to "invigorate" the Natchez Jewish community, and a new effort to build a temple began. Ullman served on the building committee, which soon purchased a lot and house at the corner of Washington and Commerce streets for the sum of $500.[14]

Emma and her mother helped to organize a Ladies' Aid Society within the congregation in the fall of 1868. Mrs. Mayer served as president of the society and Emma acted as secretary. Dues of one dollar a year were collected and, in a clever and possibly mocking stroke (since women were not allowed full privileges at that time in Reform temples), the society resolved in its constitution and bylaws that "any gentleman of the Jewish faith may be permitted to become a member of the Society, but shall not be entitled to any vote, or take any action in the meeting of the Society, neither can he be elected to any office."[15] In 1869 the Hebrew Ladies' Aid Society voted to give the congregation $3,875 they had raised through church fairs, a remarkable accomplishment that received recognition and approval in the local newspapers. This action spurred the building program forward, and by January 1870 construction on the temple began.[16]

Although Ullman's energetic leadership led to progress on the building of a temple, his presidency was not without controversy. He complained at length in quarterly and annual reports of the poor attendance of the congregants at temple services, of the lack of payment of dues, of parental indifference toward the Sunday school program, and of disputes among members of the congregation. He saved his few words of praise for the women of the congregation who, he said, served "indefatigably." His "progressive ideas roused some opposition"; "rumblings of disaffection" arose over construction details, the choice of a rabbi, and the mode or style of worship to be followed. Despite such problems, construction of the temple continued, and a dedication ceremony was held on March 8, 1872, preceded the night before by a "Grand Masquerade and Fancy Dress Ball." Ullman served on the committees that planned both of these events.[17]

In 1875 and again in 1878 Ullman served as interim lay rabbi for the congregation. During those terms and on other occasions, Ullman usually chose to lecture on popular rather than theological subjects. His sermons reflected his humor, intellect, and philosophy of life. In a lecture delivered on the occasion of Rosh Hashanah in 1877, Ullman lightheartedly inquired of the congregation about the motivations that had brought them to synagogue that day. He proposed several possible answers, then continued, "It cannot be the love of pleasure since if it afforded you great or even little gratification to resort to the sanctuary of the Most High, there to pour forth your feelings of devotion, gratitude, and adoration, we would not be compelled throughout the rest of the year to look upon a desert of empty benches." In the same sermon Ullman revealed his philosophy of time, life, and service. He developed the theme of counting or claiming one's days:

> The earth and all her fullness, the sun, moon, and planets, the innumerable stars that nightly deck the canopy of heaven are but the garden planted by the hand of God on the shores of time and we through the love of God were called from the womb of time and placed in this world garden. We were endowed with the majesty of

reason and the divine power of free will. We were bid to conquer and subdue time and out of its vast materials to create a life of our own. One by one as the days pass by, to lay hold, to make them ministers to our virtues, servants to our activity, to stamp them with the ineffacable [*sic*] lives of our conduct so that when the sun sets in [the] west of our earthly career we may proudly point to them and say, "Behold, these have been our days."

In a passage that underscores Ullman's lifelong commitment to brotherhood and service, he maintained:

Wisdom is not born with man when he first sees the light of day. It is a plant of very slow growth which demands hard and continual labor. In our infancy, we must sow the seeds of truth and virtue for they mature best in the spring time of life. Daily we must remove the thorns of anger and hatred, the weeds of malice and covetousness. The good actions of our daily life are like the dew of heaven; every kindness done to a suffering fellow man is like the light of the sun, it quickens and stimulates the growth of a wise heart. The more of such rain and sunshine the riper and sweeter this fruit becomes. . . . Let us also implore God to teach us to number our days, for what avails us the tree of life, if it bears no fruit? Why pray for more days if they do not produce a wise heart and with it a change in our conduct through life?[18]

In 1870, Ullman and other temple members organized Ezra Lodge Number 134 of the International Order of B'nai B'rith, the largest Jewish organization in America. Established in 1843 by German immigrant Jews, B'nai B'rith promoted education, philanthropy, and friendship. Ullman became an active member of the local unit that met at the temple every second and fourth Sunday of the month. Both he and his business partner, David Laub, served as president of the local organization that supported orphanages in New Orleans, Louisiana, and in Cleveland, Ohio. In 1878, Ullman's popularity and leadership skills won him the presidency of B'nai B'rith's District Grand Lodge Number Seven, which comprised chapters from Texas, Arkansas, Alabama, Tennessee, Louisiana, Oklahoma, Florida, and Mississippi.[19]

The battles fought and won by Ullman at the temple must have provided good training and preparation for his service as a city alderman. Ullman sought a seat as alderman for the first ward in 1873, but failed by a vote of 123 to 74. In 1876 Ullman again ran for that office and was elected to a one-year term that began on January 1, 1877. He served on the committees on Accounts and Claims, Propositions and Licenses, Enrolled Bills, and on the Public Health Board. He ran unopposed in 1877, and during his second term took an active role in trying to obtain monies for the school teachers' fund. In 1878, Ullman handled a great deal of correspondence from people requesting information about their relatives in the area during a yellow fever epidemic that developed in New Orleans and moved up the river. Ullman received the inquiries because of his dual positions as a member of Natchez's Board of Health and as president of B'nai B'rith's regional district grand lodge. Many residents of Natchez, including Ullman's family, moved north of the city to escape the "plague." The rabbi of B'nai Israel fled, as did Ullman's brother-in-law Henry Frank, who left his business in Ullman's charge. Thus Ullman ran his own business and that of his brother-in-law, served as interim lay leader of the temple, acted as sanitary inspector for one-fourth of the city, and presided over B'nai B'rith business. He must have seen something of himself in the words he wrote to a friend in New Orleans who was going through similar difficult times: "Your large heart does not listen to the complaints of your overtaxed body. . . . It has often been a question with me which of the two, your head or the heart is most active. Thanks to you and permit me in the name of our common humanity to thank you that you have the disposition to execute what the one contemplates." Ullman felt his own efforts repaid when he reported in September 1878 that his "dear little city" had escaped the epidemic because of the quarantine and sanitary regulations he helped to enforce.[20]

Ullman lost his bid for reelection in 1879. When his term of office expired, the Board of Aldermen passed a resolution on January 1, 1880 stating that during Ullman's service as an alderman, he and another retiring alderman "endeared themselves to the members of the Board by their uniform courtesy in debate, their manly bearing and the wisdom and prudence which has ever characterized them during their respective terms of office." The loss of their services "bears not lightly upon our citizens at large who have ever profited by their sound judgment and calm discretion in the management of city affairs."[21]

Ullman, however, was not long idle or absent from community affairs. He became a member of the Board of Visitors of the Natchez Institute in 1881, appointed by the mayor and aldermen to act as a modern-day board of education in exercising supervision over both the white Natchez Institute and the black Union School. The Board of Visitors did just that: members visited the schools to observe teacher and student deportment, building and supply needs, and grounds maintenance. They hired teachers for one-year terms, and often chose to rehire the existing "corps of teachers." The board established salaries at the white Natchez Institute in 1882 at forty dollars a month for teachers, with the principal earning one hundred dollars a month. Teachers at the black Union School also received forty dollars a month; the principal there earned seventy-five dollars.[22]

Members of the Board of Visitors also made curriculum decisions, requiring students in 1881 to purchase the "revised McGuffey series." As grade levels were added to the Natchez Institute, the board ordered the principal to organize advanced classes in "geometry, algebra, rhetoric, composition and other branches usually taught in high school." At the end of each year's school term, Ullman participated in giving oral examinations to students to determine their level of competency, and the board published the results of those oral exams in the local newspaper.[23]

In response to a complaint of a teacher against three students for "misdemeanors in the schoolroom," Ullman and other members of the Board of Visitors required the children and their parents to appear before them to explain the behavior before the students could rejoin the class. One of the accused presented himself and made a "candid and manly confession and expression of regret," reporting that he had already apologized to the teacher. He was reinstated immediately. The second culprit's father appeared with an acceptable excuse for his son's absence and his hearing was postponed. The third student failed to appear or send an excuse, and he was summarily suspended.[24]

When Ullman resigned as a trustee of Union School, a post that came with his service on the Board of Visitors, the teachers and principal of that school issued a resolution of tribute to him. The document expressed the black employees' "superlative appreciation" for Ullman's courtesy, his "uniform impartiality," and "general disposition" in his attempts to "transmit the rays of intelligence to the minds of 450 pupils, the crude material out [of] which must come factors [sic] to the future American citizenship."[25]

Ullman resigned his position on the Board of Visitors in early 1884 because he was moving his family to Birmingham, Alabama. He regularly returned to Natchez to visit family and friends. In 1905, when he was sixty-five, Ullman was the featured speaker at a service dedicating a newly constructed temple for B'nai Israel.[26]

During the Natchez years, Ullman reached middle age. He established a family, managed a business, and honed his natural gifts as a civic, religious, and educational leader. He earned the admiration and appreciation of the people of Natchez for his contributions to the community. Even greater opportunities for service awaited Ullman in Birmingham.

CHAPTER 4

The Birmingham Years: Educator

Ullman, like the thousands of others who flooded into Birmingham in the 1880s, expected to find exciting new economic opportunities in the thirteen-year-old city. Between 1880 and 1890 the city grew in population from 3,086 to approximately 26,178. Such rapid growth created many problems, among them inadequate fire and police protection, insufficient water supplies, and too few schools. The city became "the most criminal city of her size in the nation," with crimes occurring in spots with such exotic names as Beer Mash, Buzzard Roost, and Scratch Ankle. But problems also offered opportunities for effective leadership, and Samuel Ullman's innate gifts and Natchez experiences equipped him in a special way for civic and religious leadership in Birmingham.[1]

"New South" Birmingham seemed to hold unlimited prospects for those who chose it as home. "Nowhere in the world did things happen as they happened in Birmingham," one observer of the 1880s noted. Men made trades before breakfast and "property changed hands as much as four and five times a day." "A brand new sensation was born everyday." Still, historian C. Vann Woodward suggested that Birmingham was a "speculator's town . . . throttled first by cholera and then by the alternate diseases that have beset it all its days — depression and boom." The Ullmans arrived in the spring of 1884 just as Birmingham suffered one of those regularly occurring, albeit temporary, depressions in its economy.[2]

In the midst of economic uncertainty, Ullman moved his

family into a residence located at 715 North Eighteenth Street and opened the Ullman Hardware Company at 1808–1810 Second Avenue. Ullman became one of about five thousand foreign-born citizens who lived in Birmingham in 1890. There was a sufficient population of German-Americans, the third largest white ethnic group in Birmingham after the English and Scotch, to support several breweries and German-language newspapers in the city through the 1890s. The city's white population represented approximately sixty percent of the total, and most of the white population resided in houses that nestled in Jones Valley. Blacks, who comprised forty percent of the city's population, usually lived in poorly constructed, poorly ventilated cottages often located in alleyways.[3]

Ullman's Hardware Company advertised mill, mine, and furnace supplies, building materials, sash, blinds, paint, glass, oils, and general hardware. City records reveal a permanency about the Ullman home but a puzzling and unexplained instability in the housing of the hardware company. The store moved from its Second Avenue location in 1888 to 218–220 Nineteenth Street, then in 1890 to 2013 Third Avenue. Despite the city's expanding commerce, Ullman's business apparently provided barely adequate income for his family, so he became involved in other business ventures. He served on the board of directors of the Birmingham National Bank, and in March 1887 he helped to incorporate and became president of the Lakeside Land Company, with offices located at 115 Twenty-first Street.[4]

Ullman's business interests never thrived; he never achieved a position of wealth. Unable to be philanthropic without money, he invested his energy and experience tirelessly to many of the best causes and purposes in Birmingham. During the Gilded Age and beyond, Birmingham was a city in which "success," social prestige, and power within the community were usually won and measured by pragmatism, deal making, and money. Ullman, however, achieved influence in Birmingham by the force of his personality, integrity, and energy. Yet even as he became an important actor in the economic, religious, and civic life of Birmingham, he, as other Jewish merchants, was excluded from the elite social clubs of the city.[5]

Only months before the Ullmans arrived in Alabama, the mayor and aldermen of Birmingham, hired a young educator from Ohio, John Herbert Phillips, to organize and superintend the city's public schools. Proprietary schools (nonsectarian and open to the public) for both races had been established earlier by private interests and subsequently were taken over by the city. In 1884, the Alabama legislature took the direct administration of the city's schools away from the mayor and aldermen and ordered that control of schools be given to an "independent" Board of Education appointed by the mayor and aldermen. The city, through its Board of Aldermen, continued to provide funds for the city's schools but no longer had a direct role in educational policy. The Board of Aldermen appointed one of the city's newest arrivals, Samuel Ullman, to serve as a member on this first Board of Education for the city of Birmingham. Drawing upon the experience he had gained in Natchez, Ullman remained on the board without interruption from 1884 through 1900 and again from 1902 to 1904. He served as president of the board from 1893 to 1900. Together with Phillips, Ullman helped to create a program later judged to be "one of the best systems of schools in the country."[6]

While Ullman's service on the board ultimately became controversial, his initial service often seemed dull and mundane. He served on a committee to purchase furniture for the public schools, and members of the board chose Ullman to chair the Committee on Instruction. He recommended the adoption of written rules and regulations to govern both pupils and faculty, and he compiled a list of textbooks to be used in the schools. He joined with the board in 1884 in establishing the salaries of white teachers at fifty dollars a month, with black teachers to be paid thirty-five dollars.[7]

Ullman recommended favorable action on a proposal submitted by Birmingham's German Society that the German language be taught in the public schools. Its easy passage reflected not only Ullman's German antecedents, but also suggests the size and influence of the city's German population in the 1880s and 1890s. Oddly, the teaching of German indirectly caused a minor controversy for Ullman and the board when, in 1888, parents of students taking the German language course accused the teacher, Leon Landsberg, of being a socialist who also held anarchistic beliefs. Landsberg admitted his socialist leanings, denied being an anarchist, and might have kept his job had he not also been accused of habitually frequenting a local saloon. He resigned under fire.[8]

Ullman's Committee on Instruction established procedures for examining teachers before their employment and established various levels of certification for principals, teachers, and instructors in special areas like music and language arts. Under these rules prospective teachers were examined in the theory and practice of teaching, orthography (spelling), reading, grammar, penmanship, rhetoric, history, Latin, geology, astronomy, physiology, and algebra. A teaching candidate earned a three-year certificate for answering ninety percent of the questions correctly, whereas a seventy percent level earned a candidate only a one-year certificate.[9]

In 1886 the board rejected the idea of allowing nonresident students to attend city schools without paying additional fees. Board members became "visitors" to each school in the system, where they checked and reported on conditions. Ullman became the visitor for the former West End School, which recently had been renamed the Robert H. Henley School to honor the city's first mayor. After visiting the Henley School in late 1886, Ullman reported everything there to be satisfactory except for the need to improve and fence in the grounds around the school. In an ecumenical move, Ullman recommended at the April 5, 1887 meeting of the board that Good Friday be made a legal school holiday, and the board approved his motion. However, in an earlier, somewhat related decision, the board turned down Ullman's request that a Jewish congregation be allowed to use one of its schools for meetings. As a result of the debate, the board passed a general resolution that established the principle that school facilities were "strictly for city school purposes."[10]

At Phillips's request, Ullman in November 1888 recommended moving the German language offering from the seventh- and eighth-grade curriculum to the high school level. No action was taken on this proposal, but the question of how much and at what level to teach German continued to be raised through August 1889 when Ullman's motion was defeated. The German community actively resisted the move despite Ullman's assurances that no educational benefits were being lost by the change.[11]

In January 1889 members of the board chose Ullman to be its vice president, a position he held while continuing to serve on the Committee on Instruction and as visitor to the Henley School. Later that year he became chairman of a special committee to review teacher salaries. The committee reported with regret that the board had no revenue from which to recommend salary increases. In April Ullman offered a resolution that the board passed and sent to city officials recommending that the city donate $5,000 to match $5,000 already raised by the "public spirited citizens of Birmingham" to create a public library. He further suggested that the library be housed, initially, in one of the city's schools, and be exclusively controlled by the Board of Education. Phillips's annual report to the board that year disclosed overcrowding in all city schools but particularly in black schools, where teacher-pupil ratios ran as high as 53 to 1 at Slater School and 74 to 1 at Lane School; at East End School, one teacher tried "to manage, not to teach" 125 pupils.[12]

While Ullman served as vice president of the board in

1891, three telephones were installed in selected schools. Rules for the use of these miracle instruments became necessary, so board members decided that "no teachers shall be allowed to use the telephone during school hours," and principals were charged with taking and delivering all messages. In 1892, Ullman led in establishing a corps of substitute teachers, and he joined the board in abolishing tuition charges at the high school level as they had been abolished in the lower grades.[13]

In January 1893, members of the Board of Education elected Ullman to be their president, and although his influence on that board grew proportionately, the timing of this honor was not fortuitous. The economic depression that gripped the nation affected Birmingham in a particularly grim fashion. As unemployed workers left the city to search for work elsewhere, the student population in some areas of the city declined, while new schools were needed for students in recently annexed neighborhoods like North and South Highlands. Initially, Ullman's new status allowed him to succeed, finally, in having German language studies moved from grammar school level to the high school. In July 1893, he successfully, although temporarily, resisted a move to shorten the school term from nine to eight months as a cost-saving effort. But financial problems plagued the city's schools, leading Phillips to reduce his own salary voluntarily in 1893 rather than reduce teacher salaries.[14]

Economic constraints eventually forced Ullman and the board to postpone the opening of city schools in 1894 from September to October and to reinstate tuition charges of two dollars per month at the high school, which made that school almost self-sustaining. By December 1894 economic conditions had worsened and Ullman, with board approval, reduced the salaries of the principals at both white and "colored" schools by twenty percent. At one point during the economic difficulties of the nineties, the board used Ullman's association with banker Sigfried Steiner to borrow monies from the Steiner Brothers Bank to meet teacher payrolls. By the late 1890s, Birmingham's school system finally recovered from its financial problems. Teacher salaries stabilized so that experienced white teachers received between $360 and $450 annually, while black teachers' salaries ranged from $225 to $450.[15]

Superintendent Phillips, in his 1893 annual report to the board, chose to contrast prevailing conditions with those that had existed in 1883 when he became superintendent. He reminded the citizens of Birmingham that the city system began in 1884 with one white and one black school, fifteen teachers, and 1,515 students. Phillips and Ullman were proud to report in 1893 that, despite the city's economic woes, the system now had eight schools, ninety-three teachers, and 10,124 students. As impressive as these figures were, Ullman continued to voice concern about the problem of classroom overcrowding that was particularly bad in several grades within the "colored" schools. His concern led to employment of two additional teachers for those schools.[16]

Many decisions relating to public education during this era revolved in Birmingham, as throughout much of the South, around the issue of providing for blacks education that was separate and, perhaps, distinct from that offered to whites. The Reconstruction dream of blacks to gain an education that would equip them to join a new social order in which they would stand equal with whites was not to be attained easily. Segregation of the races occurred, either through custom or legal mandate, even before the U.S. Supreme Court confirmed it in the 1896 *Plessy v. Ferguson* decision. Debate over the merits and content of education for blacks was heated and long. Southern industry's requirement of cheap, common laborers seemed to many in the South to suggest the need for, at most, a limited, vocational education for blacks, an education based "solely upon the contribution which it could make to greater industrial productivity." Educational "reformers" in the late-19th-century South, however, believed that a blend of academic and vocational schooling could and would improve the behavior, health, moral values, discipline, and efficiency of workers, black and white, without requiring or causing race or class lines to be crossed.[17]

Ullman fearlessly, almost innocently, placed himself in the forefront of the debate in Birmingham over the nature and extent of educational opportunities to be offered to blacks in the city. He subscribed to a mixture of academic and industrial education for both black and white students. Such a consistently moderate view placed him in a controversial position among more militant and extremist elements within the community. His was by no means the universally held position in the nation, state, or city. The *Montgomery Advertiser* expressed an alternate view in a 1900 editorial: "The undeniable truth is that the Negro is not fitted to perform successfully any work which requires skill, patience, or mental capacity. There is something lacking in their brain [*sic*] and in their body [*sic*]. Their minds cannot comprehend the intricacies of fine mechanical work and their hands cannot be trained to accomplish it."[18] For many in Birmingham, providing any education for blacks was an unnecessary expense at best, and at worst placed blacks in a more competitive position to take jobs from whites.

Ullman's friend and associate, Phillips, was one of few progressive urban school administrators in the South who believed that the "enlightened selfishness of white southerners as well as their sense of duty, should lead them to provide public schooling for black children." Between 1883 and 1887, during Ullman's early years on the board, Birmingham built adequate and similar frame school buildings for both races. The improvement in black facilities was credited with leading to increased black enrollment and attendance. Between 1887 and 1891 school construction continued, but brick structures began to be built for whites, while black schools continued to be of frame construction. Between 1900 and 1907 only schools for white students were constructed, a state of affairs caused, in part, by the waning influence of Ullman and finally by his absence from the Board of Education after 1904.[19]

Ullman's interest in and concern for the scope and availability of education for the city's black children began during his earliest days on the board. In 1885 he worked out a course of study for a proposed night school for blacks who, because of their employment, could not attend day schools. Later the question of technical and vocational training for blacks and the desire of blacks within the city to have their own high school became much-debated and often controversial issues. Ullman carefully studied the curricula offered in other industrial cities and, as early as 1887, he advocated that drawing classes and other technical courses be incorporated into the Birmingham curriculum. The board approved a commercial course for the high school in 1891, but this, of course, affected only whites since blacks had no high school.[20]

In 1896 the board, with Ullman at its helm, forcefully recommended to both the mayor and the superintendent that they aggressively fund industrial training in the Negro schools. Ullman continued into 1899 to argue for the addition of manual training in the existing grades of black schools. The board should broaden the curriculum offered blacks, he said, "to improve the possibilities of our colored children, recognizing that . . . nearly all our domestic help are colored, and as such are in daily contact with our children; hence the duty of raising their moral standard [is] indicated as much as their educational standard." Such statements, while troubling today, fit the progressive social consciousness of the late nineteenth century. In that context Ullman's views were both pragmatic and progressive. "We should do this [add manual training to the black school curriculum]," said Ullman, "because it pays, both morally and pecuniarily. Schools," he argued, "can be maintained cheaper than penal institutions. An educated heart and hand is better adapted to overcome vice than simple so-called book learning."[21]

Ullman's advocacy of technical courses for black students persisted and grew to giving unprecedented support to the creation of a high school for blacks in Birmingham. For many years, blacks had requested that additional grades be added to at least one of their schools until they, too, had a high school. In June 1900, a group of black citizens led by Arthur H. Parker, a teacher and later principal of the city's first black high school, asked to meet with the board. Their purpose was "to request the Board of Education to establish a High School for Negroes." Parker recalled that "Dr. Samuel Ullman was chairman of the Board and encouraged the movement," which enjoyed Phillips's somewhat weaker support. Ullman's endorsement was uncommon, as indicated by the fact that sixteen years later the states of Georgia, Mississippi, South Carolina, and Louisiana still had no four-year high schools for blacks even though the black secondary-school-age population of those states exceeded fifty percent of the total school-age population.[22]

In Birmingham's experience, Ullman's support was "crucial," but, from a personal point of view, the battle for a black high school could hardly have occurred at a worse time. In 1901 Alabama's governor, William Samford, called a constitutional convention with the announced purpose of finding a way to "reform" Alabama's suffrage process, a process fraught with corruption particularly during the 1890s. Suggesting that efforts to manipulate and control black voters caused most of the corruption, the state's politicians debated various ways to "legally" disfranchise blacks. One of easiest ways to discourage black voter participation in a state where over a third of the population could neither read nor write was to require that voters be literate.

A distinguished Samuel Ullman, circa 1900, at about sixty years of age. (Photograph courtesy of Mayer U. Newfield.)

For Ullman vigorously to defend the expansion and improvement of educational opportunities for blacks when literacy was needed in order for them to gain the vote was exceedingly dangerous ground for him to tread. He nonetheless pressed his support for a high school for blacks despite the bitter disfranchisement campaign and the opposition of key white political leaders in Birmingham. His support proved crucial. Industrial High School for black students opened in the fall of 1900 as one room on the second floor of the Cameron Elementary School. Eighteen students marked the first day of attendance at the new "school" with "grateful prayers," singing, and celebration. The black community had won their high school with financial support "well above [the] traditional black level" through the joint persistence and cooperation of black leaders and white community progressives, among whom Ullman was clearly the most influential.[23]

Ullman's support for a high school for black students was not without its cost. "It has never been a popular course of action for white men in the South to stand up for the rights of Negroes," wrote an observer of the region. "At no time in the South's history has this been more true than in the period of roughly 1885–1917."[24] The deep opposition of key white political leaders was obvious when members of the Board of Aldermen, a board on which Ullman himself served from 1895 to 1897, were so angered by Ullman's actions that they refused to reelect him to the Board of Education in 1900. Ullman was off the board, albeit, briefly, for the first time since 1884. An editorial in the [Birmingham] *Age-Herald* on January 20, 1901 said, "The people of this town are debtors to Samuel Ullman, inasmuch as he gave eighteen years of service to the public serving them with rare devotion, enthusiasm, and unselfishness, without recovering one cent of pay. He was turned out of office unexpectedly, and Mayor [Walter M.]

Drennen admits that a mistake was made by the Board of Aldermen."[25]

In November 1900, Ullman's supporters, including Mayor Drennen and Superintendent Phillips, succeeded in having a newly constructed elementary school for whites at Sixth Avenue and Twelfth Street South named for Ullman. The Samuel Ullman School opened in the fall of 1901. Ullman was reappointed to the Board of Education in 1902 and served through 1904, but his stature and influence on that board was greatly diminished.[26]

Until the end of his tenure on the board, Ullman maintained an almost revolutionary outspokenness regarding the need for adequate and improved educational opportunities for both black and white children. For twenty years during important developmental years, Ullman led the way in creating teacher certification standards, helping to establish a public library, developing a corps of substitute teachers, pressing for building and grounds improvements, being the voice of fair play and high standards in the city's black and white schools. By 1905, he no longer served on that board and his well-known "sympathy for the weak and helpless" was clearly missing. His absence was almost immediately felt when, late in 1905, blacks petitioned the Board of Education for better facilities and were told that their request was both ill-advised and insulting.[27]

The Samuel Ullman School at Twelfth Street and Seventh Avenue South opened in the fall of 1901 as an elementary school for white children. In 1937, it was converted into a high school for black students, and in 1971 it became a part of The University of Alabama at Birmingham, where it now houses the School of Social and Behavioral Sciences. (Photograph courtesy of The University of Alabama at Birmingham.)

This plaque of Ullman originally hung in the Samuel Ullman Library of the Hebrew Young Men's Association building in Birmingham. When that organization ceased to exist, the plaque was moved to the Ullman Building on the campus of The University of Alabama at Birmingham, where it still hangs. Note that the plaque incorrectly gives the date of Ullman's birth as 1841. (Photograph courtesy of The University of Alabama at Birmingham.)

Another view of the Ullman Building, showing the wing that was added in 1957 to meet the needs of a growing population of black students when it served as a high school. (Photograph courtesy of The University of Alabama at Birmingham.)

CHAPTER 5

The Birmingham Years: Rabbi

Ullman's concern and care for society's most vulnerable groups was shared by his wife Emma, a devoted companion and mother, a source of poetic inspiration for Ullman, and an active player in Birmingham's Jewish and civic communities. She and Ullman helped to create Hillman Hospital, which began to operate in 1888 as a charity hospital for the city, and both served actively on its Board of Managers. One floor of the Hughes Building on Twentieth Street was leased for the facility, and Emma helped to choose and purchase furnishings for the thirty-six-bed hospital. She served on the hospital's governing board until her death after a brief illness in 1896. The community eulogized Emma Ullman in the Birmingham *State Herald* as "the center and inspiration not only of an ideal family of cultured and refined people, but of a large circle of admiring and devoted friends." John Herbert Phillips described her as an "effective and sympathetic partner of her husband," and extolled her as "foremost in every charity, esteemed by rich and poor as one of the truest and best of women" in the community. Her sudden death on March 4 devastated Ullman, who never remarried.[1]

The decade of the 1890s challenged Ullman with enormous changes. Elevated to the presidency of the Board of Education, Ullman served a term as city alderman, suffered financial reverses in his hardware business, sat on civic and commercial boards, and, at the encouragement of his good friend and colleague Phillips, helped to establish and served on the board of one of the first southern chapters of the

American Society for the Prevention of Cruelty to Animals. In addition, in a unique and unprecedented action in American Judaism, Ullman moved in 1893 from lay president of Birmingham's Temple Emanu-El to become its spiritual leader and lay rabbi.[2]

The first Jews arrived in Birmingham around 1871, shortly after the city was incorporated. The Simons arrived in 1871, the Marxes in 1873, and the Hochstadters in 1874. A formal congregation began to meet in June 1882 with thirty-two charter members, half of whom were single young men. Between 1883 and 1885 many more Jews came into Birmingham, swelling the ranks of the small congregation and causing it to think of building its own place of worship. "The most notable addition to the congregational life [of Temple Emanu-El] was the coming of Samuel Ullman in the spring of 1884." His experience in the religious and civic life of Natchez and his "fervid enthusiasm" and charisma brought Ullman instantly to a "commanding position" in the Birmingham congregation. Almost immediately upon joining the congregation, Ullman began to officiate at Sabbath and Holy Day services. In 1886, the congregation further recognized his important place among them by electing him president of Emanu-El. As president, he made the primary address at the ceremony laying the cornerstone of the first temple at Seventeenth Street and Fifth Avenue North on July 31, 1886. One observer noted that Ullman delivered this speech in his "peculiarly happy style."[3]

Ullman's presidential report in 1887 sketched the history of the congregation during the previous year and offered thanks to God for "manifest blessings," not the least of which, Ullman asserted, was the unanimous election of Maurice Eisenberg to be rabbi of the Emanu-El congregation. Temple construction was completed, new members joined the congregation, and Ullman encouraged the growing membership to support Rabbi Eisenberg in building the Sunday school

Samuel and Emma Ullman were among the founders of Birmingham's first hospital, which later became Hillman Hospital, and served for years on its governing and managing boards. The University of Alabama at Birmingham Medical Center is an outgrowth of Hillman Hospital. (Photograph courtesy of The University of Alabama at Birmingham.)

The original building of Temple Emanu-El, located on the southwest corner of Seventeenth Street and Fifth Avenue North. Ullman was member, president, and ultimately rabbi of this congregation. (Photograph courtesy of the Department of Archives and Manuscripts, Birmingham Public Library.)

program. He also praised Eisenberg's work with the temple choir, which "Mr. Eisenberg is so eminently well-qualified to take charge of." Ullman also recommended paying the congregation's secretary eight percent of collections for his services and, finally, expressed his "heartfelt and sincere thanks" for the congregation's support and confidence. "My humble efforts would have availed me but little had you not given me your support and ready and cheerful assistance. I claim nothing for myself except that I have tried to do my duty[,] no man can do more." After nine resignations and eight suspensions for nonpayment of dues, the congregation consisted in 1887 of ninety-three members who paid Rabbi Eisenberg $2,000 per annum. In that same year, the congregation reelected Ullman to be its president for another term.[4]

At the March 18, 1888 meeting of the Board of Trustees of the temple, Eisenberg brought a complaint against the temple organist who, prior to Eisenberg's coming, had directed the choir. Ullman and the Board of Trustees notified the organist that in the future he should consider himself "as being under the control of our Rabbi." On June 3, 1888 Eisenberg was unanimously reelected rabbi and given a salary increase, but soon afterward the choir requested the temple board to withdraw Eisenberg as leader of the choir and to turn control entirely over to Mr. Franklin, the organist. "We find it absolutely impossible to follow two leaders," members of the choir told the board. The board complied with the choir's request and sent a note to Eisenberg informing him of the change. At the same time, membership doubled and Eisenberg's discharge of his duties appeared to be most successful. In April 1889 the church organist resigned and a succession of organist-choir directors followed. Other issues that concerned the congregation included nonpayment of dues and the need for cemetery improvements. In the fall of 1889 the congregation, by acclamation, reelected Ullman, who appeared to deal directly with each problem as it arose.[5]

But a major controversy stirred within the congregation. In the spring of 1890, a member of the Emanu-El congregation accused Rabbi Eisenberg of "improper and lascivious behavior" toward his wife. A committee of five chaired by Ullman was created to hear the charges as well as Eisenberg's defense, and all parties agreed that the committee's decision would be final. A certain Mr. and Mrs. Fox charged that while Eisenberg gave Mrs. Fox lessons on Judaism and prepared her for membership in the congregation, his behavior became improper toward her. The committee unanimously declared Eisenberg innocent of the charges. Eisenberg's actions, declared the board on April 20, 1890, were "at that time, as they always have been, chaste and pure." Later that month, Eisenberg was reelected rabbi by an overwhelming vote.[6]

The issue did not go away, the gossip continued, and on May 18 the board met to respond to Eisenberg's resignation. The board voted five to four to accept the resignation with Ullman voting against accepting the resignation. A congregational meeting held later that day erupted into lengthy and emotional debate. In a vote of the congregation, sixty-six members voted to accept the rabbi's resignation, while sixty-seven voted to reject it and to retain Eisenberg as spiritual leader. A deeply divided congregation continued to debate Eisenberg's future, and he won another narrow victory in a congregational vote taken on June 29. On July 1 nineteen members formally resigned to form a new congregation. Among those resigning was Phillip Fox. Later in July, Ullman and the board granted Eisenberg a four-week leave of absence, but he continued to hold the position of rabbi.[7]

In the midst of this crisis, financial problems foreshadowing the Panic of 1893 began to surface. Paid choir members received notification that their services were no longer needed and that after August 1 a volunteer choir would be attempted. On August 31 the board ordered Ullman to notify Eisenberg that the congregation "might be unable to pay the full amount" previously set as his salary and requesting from him a written statement of the salary he required to continue as rabbi of the congregation. Eisenberg responded that, although his salary was set at $2,000 per annum, he would serve for nothing. The congregation voted to pay him at least $1,200 per annum and as much above that as they could raise. All of this became moot a few days later when on September 3 the Board of Trustees accepted Eisenberg's second resignation effective November 1. Immediate steps toward reunification began with those who left the congregation over the Fox affair as Ullman and others encouraged those who left to return to Emanu-El. Eisenberg, whose innocence the board still maintained, was given an honorary membership in the congregation.[8]

There are, of course, modern implications in the Eisenberg affair. Max Samfield, editor of the *Jewish Spectator*, corresponded with Ullman during the controversy and agreed with Ullman's position that improper behavior had not been proven and that Eisenberg could not be found guilty on the testimony of only one witness. Nonetheless, Samfield argued, Eisenberg demonstrated poor judgment when he taught the lady under the "promise of secrecy" which gave the appearance of "stealth and clandestiness [*sic*]." Eisenberg compounded this error in judgment by teaching Mrs. Fox at the temple rather than at his home where (by inference) Eisenberg's wife would have been present. One can only speculate about the significance of the board's recommendation to the congregation in December 1890 that Dr. Aaron Hahn of Cleveland, Ohio be elected to serve as rabbi at a salary of $2,400 a year, when they had informed Eisenberg so recently of their inability to pay him his full salary.[9]

When the congregation was asked on December 7, 1890 to ratify the recommendation of the board to call Dr. Hahn as rabbi, they refused. Instead, over his objection, the congregation "elected Mr. Samuel Ullman [rabbi] unanimously for a term of two years at a salary of $2,400 p. annum." Ullman soon accepted and later said that the unsought and unanimous call would "always be a source of pride and pleasure to me." He remained humble and pragmatic about his call to serve as lay rabbi of Temple Emanu-El, declaring, "Having failed in business, I suppose was the main reason that called me to that exalted position." While he was pleased and honored at his selection, Ullman always felt that his lack of formal education left him ill-prepared for the job.[10]

Several observers have suggested that "this transference of a layman from the worldly [administrative] to the spiritual leadership of a congregation" was a "unique incident in the congregational life of American Judaism." In this difficult position, as in his tenure on the school board, Ullman's ability, integrity, and personality combined to see the congregation through enormously difficult days. The dissension created over the Eisenberg affair did not quickly dissipate, and temple membership growth continued to be stagnant. Ullman's message to the congregation in August 1891 acknowledged a lack of growth, but noted that services were well-attended and that harmony within the congregation had been restored. He introduced new programs like the one to improve participation in the Sunday school by awarding medals that encouraged scholarship in the Sunday school program. His efforts were recognized by the president of the temple who congratulated the congregation in 1891 for having had the

wisdom to place in their pulpit, to teach and advise us, as our Rabbi, our oft tried and self-sacrificing friend, our efficient and earnest co-worker in the cause of Isreal [sic], our guide through the sea of discord that only a short while ago threatened to engulf our Congregation. That this selection was a wise one, every member of this Congregation knows, and has reasons to feel proud of; and today I want to congratulate you upon the peaceful and harmonious condition of our affairs, brought about by the advise and council [sic] and pleading of our true friend and Rabbi, Samuel Ullman. . . . Were it possible to think of anything that would in a measure compensate him for the affection which he has evidenced, individually and collectively for Congregation Emanuel, I would surely suggest it.[11]

Ullman and the congregation, while not prospering, did survive the difficult days of the 1890s. By 1893 the nationwide economic depression which had troubled the school system forced the congregation to reduce Ullman's salary. Many members requested reductions in their dues, and those requests were, of course, honored. Women were asked to become full members of the congregation in July 1893, and the congregation began, despite its financial difficulties, to send a monthly donation to the New Orleans Orphans Home.[12]

On February 11, 1894, Ullman sent the board of Temple Emanu-El his letter of resignation which was accepted with a recommendation that contributions be gathered to present as a gift to Rabbi Ullman. Ullman had led the congregation through some of its bleakest days — days of scandal followed by days of deep financial struggles. His labors as rabbi, when joined with his service on the school board and other civic activities, helped to develop the "proud reputation of the Jews of early Birmingham" as liberal, progressive, respected men of integrity.[13]

CHAPTER 6

Living Young

Upon leaving his position as lay rabbi, Ullman became an agent for the New York Life Insurance Company, a position he held until 1908 when his age and hearing loss forced him to retire. He also continued his service on the Board of Education and remained busy in a broad array of community and political activities. Along with Phillips and Sigfried Steiner of the Steiner Brothers Bank, he served as a member of the Commercial and Industrial Association of Alabama and served on that group's Committee on a Constitutional Convention. As a member both of the committee's financial and executive subcommittees, he supported a constitutional convention to write a document to replace the state's 1875 constitution. It is ironic that the constitutional convention Ullman advocated aroused the emotions and raised the issues that contributed to his having been voted off the Board of Education in 1900.[1]

After his beloved Emma's death, Ullman's twenty-two-year-old daughter Leah took over management of his house. She and Morris Newfield, who boarded with the Ullmans when he came to Temple Emanu-El as its new rabbi in 1895, had a lengthy courtship before they married in 1901. Ullman became a permanent member of their home in 1906 and resided with them at 2150 Fifteenth Avenue South until his death. He and his son-in-law enjoyed intellectual exchanges and played card games which Ullman regularly, and with great irritation, lost to Newfield. On occasion, he even played baby-sitter to his grandchildren. In 1909 he wrote Leah, who

The home of Rabbi and Mrs. Morris Newfield at 2150 15th Avenue South in Birmingham. Ullman made his home here with his daughter and her family from 1906 until his death in 1924. His room was on the second floor on the right. (Photograph courtesy of Mayer U. Newfield.)

A recent picture of the house where Ullman lived with his daughter's family at 2150 15th Avenue South. (Photograph courtesy of The University of Alabama at Birmingham.)

was convalescing in Gulfport, Mississippi from an unidenti-
fied illness, that he and Morris were caring for the children,
trying to instill "feminine qualities" in the girls and reading
stories to entertain the little ones.[2]

In 1902, Ullman fulfilled a dream when he visited Europe
for the first time since his childhood and traveled extensively
through the continent. Leah and other family members
received long, poetic letters from him in which he described
the sites he saw and the people he met. These letters, drawn
from extensive journals Ullman kept each night during his
tour, reveal a sixty-two-year-old man of energy, enthusiasm,
curiosity, and optimism about everything but the weather.
Regarding the overcast conditions he encountered, Ullman
wrote, "It is a great sacrifice in pleasure anticipated after the
expenditure of so much money to be but partially rewarded,
but even what I saw under these adverse conditions has
impressed itself upon my mind so that I can never forget this
magnificent scenery." Ullman's thorough Americanism mani-
fested itself in an observation he made in one of his letters
home: "The spirit of the past is present everywhere [in 1902
Europe] and the push, the daring, the activity — aye
recklessness — of the American is absent. The human ma-
chine (though vastly more intricate than the machine made of
iron or steel) is cheaper than that operated by steam or
electricity, and these people only take to the latter when
compelled to do so by sheer necessity."[3]

Some of the locations he visited evoked memories that
spanned five decades. The cathedrals and arcades of Stras-
bourg "revived my memory, for I had seen them over fifty
years ago, but did not appreciate the fact that they were
unusual." When he began his fifth journal he wrote that he
was tempted to call it Deuteronomy, "not because it is a
recapitulation, but rather a continuation." In Budapest he
visited his son-in-law's family and was received with great
affection and respect. At his departure an emotional farewell

took place. "Pretty soon the leave taking began and I confess that tears came to my eyes. Mrs. N[ewfield] was in tears, we kissed each other in parting and the last words that I caught as we pulled out were 'Please prevail upon Morris and Leah to come to see us.'"[4]

Back in America, Grandpa and the Newfield family regularly traveled in the summers to the cooler climate of a farm near Lake Michigan, and once a year Ullman also returned to Natchez to visit his younger brother, Marcus. Marcus's daughter-in-law remembered "Uncle Sam's" ever-present pipe from which he absentmindedly dropped ashes all over the house. Marcus always sent Ullman home with a new suit, a gift from his prosperous Ullman Clothing Store in Natchez. Ullman continued to participate in Temple Emanu-El activities, and one grandchild recalled how embarrassed he and his siblings were when their grandfather, because of his deafness, responded in an overly loud and robust voice from the seat in his regular pew at temple. Without benefit of a public address system, Ullman, at the age of seventy-four, made the major address at the dedication in March 1914 of the congregation's new edifice on Highland Avenue.[5] As an additional outlet for his creative and intellectual energies, Ullman also began to indulge more regularly in a lifelong practice of writing — letters to the editors of local newspapers about issues of the day, long and entertaining letters to friends and family, and most significantly, poetry.

On one occasion, he wrote the editor of the Birmingham *Age-Herald* an impassioned letter opposing legislation pending in Montgomery that made it all but impossible for workers in the coal mining industries of the state to recover compensation for accidents suffered on the job. Ullman categorically opposed this legislation, a position that surely won him few friends among the powerful industrial leaders in Birmingham. Alabama's coal mines experienced major explosions almost every year between 1905 and 1911, causing the deaths of

Ullman pictured with grandchildren in 1911, during one of their regular summer vacations in Petoskey, Michigan. Clockwise, from top right: Emma Newfield, Mayer Newfield, Maurice ("Reese") Rosenfield seated on stool, Lena Newfield, and Semon Newfield. Ullman holds in his right arm Lincoln Newfield and in his left arm Samuel Ullman ("Ullie") Rosenfield. (Photograph courtesy of Mayer U. Newfield.)

Ullman with grandchildren Samuel Ullman ("Ullie") Rosenfield, left, and Maurice ("Reese") Rosenfield, right, circa 1914. (Photograph courtesy of Mayer U. Newfield.)

hundreds of workers. With his usual sense of justice, fair play, and defense of the underdog, Ullman wrote, "This bill, if enacted, would more securely protect property rights, while at the same time disregard the sacredness of human life and rights."[6]

On another occasion he wrote a letter opposing a state-wide prohibition amendment that the legislature was considering. He argued that since "God has endowed us with certain desires, appetites, and passions to be indulged in reason and self-control, the abuse of these endowments is the thing to guard against. I am ready to admit that the excessive use of liquor is a great evil fraught with danger to the community at large." But he argued that the issue might cause a dangerous alliance of church and state since the 3,500 churches in Alabama could, if they wished, furnish at least ten voters each to vote for the amendment. "We regard the charge made by some of the clergy and approved by some of the press that those opposing the amendment are in league with the saloon and liquor interests as an evidence of fanatical zeal and an insult." Ullman must have been pleased and surprised when this initial attempt to make Alabama dry failed.[7]

Ullman's nephew Laurens Block, founder of the Parisian Department Store chain in Birmingham, supplied the retired but active Ullman with a desk and a secretary to take dictation and to type for him. From that desk and other locations, Ullman wrote reflective, touching poems about Judaism, Emma, the brotherhood of man, life, death, and everyday subjects drawn from his own experiences. For example, one day as Ullman walked down a Birmingham street, a friend, deep in thought, sped by him without speaking. When Ullman stopped him and inquired about what caused his haste, the friend explained that he was thinking about a business problem and was late in making an important payment on a loan. Ullman went home and penned a poem entitled, "What's Your Hurry?" On another, sadder occasion,

Ullman wrote a touching poem memorializing Laurens Block on his death. While it is not known what inspired Ullman to write "Youth," there is anecdotal evidence that it was written in 1918 during Ullman's seventy-eighth year.[8]

On his eightieth birthday, Ullman's family held a large celebration which they later marked by publishing his poetry in a collection called, *From the Summit of Years, Four Score.* His children and grandchildren — musicians, artists, teachers, attorneys, businessmen — gathered to express their love and respect for "Grandpa." Congratulatory notes poured in and the Birmingham *Ledger* wrote that Samuel Ullman — the teacher, leader, lay rabbi, public servant, and builder of schools — demonstrated "that men love, esteem, and honor those who serve with an eye single to service." John Herbert Phillips wrote his old friend a lengthy, laudatory letter that beautifully summed up Ullman's character and life. He wrote of Ullman's "noble spirit of optimism, self-sacrifice and sympathetic devotion to the highest ideals of truth and justice. . . . You have lived a triumphant life; you have no enemies to harass you; your life has risen above the plane of common hatreds and enmities, and standing on the summit of the years, you can view with some satisfaction the victories that are past, and can already hear the approving verdict of 'Well Done' from the Master of Life."[9]

Ullman died four years later on March 21, 1924 and was buried in the Jewish cemetery maintained by Temple Emanu-El on Birmingham's north side. His life in many ways redefined the meaning of "success." Forced to leave his homeland because of the persecution suffered there by Jews, he fought for the losing side during the Civil War and suffered a permanent hearing disability because of that service. He failed to achieve financial prosperity in either Natchez or Birmingham, and he spent the last quarter century of his life without the friendship and affection of his wife. But Ullman refused to be conquered by the disappointments of his life or

Ullman, at top right, with members of his sister Matilda's family who gathered for his eightieth birthday celebration. Pictured in front of the (Jewish) Phoenix Club in Birmingham in 1920, Matilda is on the second row, holding flowers. Her husband, Samuel Block, is to her left and her sons I.D. and Laurens are on the third row, far right. It was the death of Ullman's nephew Laurens Block in 1922 that inspired Ullman to write "The Passing." (Photograph courtesy of Mayer U. Newfield.)

Ullman on or near his eightieth birthday, 1920. (Photograph courtesy of Mayer U. Newfield.)

to succumb to self-pity or pessimism. He chose rather to concentrate on the love and warmth of his family, the meaning and security of his faith, and the inner satisfaction that came from service to the community. He found himself at the center of controversies, not because of a fighting spirit or a demand to be in charge, but because of his unwavering principles and convictions. He stood fearlessly, innocently, and often almost alone against prevailing opinion in advocating benefits and justice for orphans, women, blacks, and laborers. At his death Ullman was remembered for his wit, integrity, and the influence he had exerted for good. Active, alert, concerned, and involved to the end, Ullman mirrored in his life the admonitions as well as the optimism contained in his most famous literary work, "Youth."[10]

The Poems of Samuel Ullman

Samuel Ullman's poems are neither complicated nor introspective, but readers often respond to his themes from their own experience. That instant, familiar connection makes Ullman's poetry meaningful and attractive.

Ullman's habit of writing long letters, keeping journals, and putting his thoughts into poetic form was a common practice among nineteenth- and early twentieth-century Americans and Europeans. His writings are a reflection of his time as well as his disposition. His poetry, like his life, is marked by his adopted Americanism in its simplicity, democracy, and optimism. It is also distinctively Jewish — full of justice, faith, compassion, assurance of eternal life, and devotion to his Creator. There are even hints of Ullman's southernness in his poems, with their emphases on time and place in rural and natural descriptive passages.

During an era of staggering change, Ullman wrote simple, honest, conventional, but straightforward poems that flowed naturally out of a life that spanned two continents and encompassed eight decades, revolutions and wars, victories and losses. The poems are personal without being self-centered, intelligent without being academic. Goodness, love, and humor are found in Ullman's work, but also pain and serious reflection.

Ullman neglected to date most of his poems, but internal evidence suggests that many were written while he was in his seventies and eighties. Although there is a blending of topics and themes in many of his works, in this volume we have loosely organized his poems along the following lines: spiritual and religious poems (pp. 69–80); love poems to or about Emma (pp. 81–93); poems with grief and death themes (pp. 95–102); life, seasons, and nature poems (pp. 103–110); and poems that do not fall easily into any broad categories (pp. 111–124). "Youth" is found in this latter category along with "My Pipe," "What's Your Hurry?" "You and I," and others that capture, in a few lines, a spirit that encourages or lightens the mood of the reader.

SPIRITUAL AND RELIGIOUS

DESIGN OR FATE?

Methinks that life is more than Creed,
   Is more than dust or craving lust.
Are hopes but dreams that fail in need,
   That fly away like mist and dust?

I weep and mourn and deeply grieve,
   With toiling souls in their distress;
And in the *tramp* that ne'er achieves
   I find myself in other dress.

Justice, must be made the base of life;
   And those men dwarfed be made whole;
Come! let the bugle end the strife,
   And let the world get back its soul.

Let us not shrink in days of pain,
   And let's not wait another day,
But we'll strike now, e'er [sic] it be vain,
   Put on your armor, end the fray.

I do not think we're led by Fate,
   A great design is being wrought,
Which will not end, till full estate,
   Reveals to us one only God.

THY TRACE

Thou Infinite, I see thy trace,
In sun and moon, in starlight face,
In royal oak and tiny seed,
In prattling babe and creeping weed.
In hours of doubt, and lowering cloud,

With thanks and praise I sing aloud.
With hope at bay, held back by fear,
I raise my voice, for thou art near.
Say not that God doth dwell afar,
On land and sea, where'er we are
In darkest hour He gives us cheer; —
I have no doubts, I feel He's near.

"MARS AND MAMMON"
With apologies to Julian A. Dubois

"Who said the ancient gods were dead?
    Who rejoiced at the obsequies?
Two rule the world today
    And riot in our miseries."

"The one fierce resolute and vain,
    With terror dripping from his hands,
Marshals our youth to untimely death,
    And sears the fruitage of our lands."

"The other wily and cunningly
    Spins 'round our souls a golden web,
Exults to note, 'mid wild protest
    As our high ideals slowly ebb."

And where, I ask, twixt this mighty twain
    Shall God our Father find a place?
What boots it that our lips proclaim
    The God of Love, the God of Grace.

Our deeds belie our work and words,
    We laud these powers and homage pay,

Their "Greed and Graft" has blinded us,
   We are their shackled slaves today.

The God of Justice does exist,
   He will rise up from blood drunk sod —
These gods we have, ourselves we made,
   Judean spoke — "There is one GOD."

ISRAEL — THE DREAMER

The food economist in Joseph —
The sociologist in Moses —
The great soldier in Joshuah —
The priestess leader in Deborah —
The melodious poet in David —
The wise moralist in Koheleth.
The profound philosopher in Job,
The spiritual poet in Isaiah,
The ethical teacher in Micah,
The seer in the prophet of Naz'reth,
A Sabbath day for the free and bonded,
The appeal for liberty in all lands,
The crime of withholding Labor's wage,
Upon his banner inscribed:
"Hear Israel, Yah our God is one!"

He fought and won from Egypt's king,
He fought and lost to Syria's host,
He slaved and mourned on Tigris' strand;
With zealous trust, took staff in hand,
Rebuilt the Temple on Zion's mound.
Reaffirming his fealty to Jacob's God
He restrung his lyre, entoning new psalms.
He again voiced the Oneness of God,

He defeated the malice of Haman,
He felled the hosts of Antiochus —
He succumbed to the legions of Rome —
He was burned and crucified in Spain;
He rose and fell like Tides in the Sea.

He dreamt and wept by Babylon's stream,
On its willows hanged his harp, and said:
"If I forget thee Jerusalem,
Let my right hand forget its cunning."
He sang and rejoiced at Sinai's slopes,
He dreamt and wept on the Rhine and Rhone,
He strove and failed in Castilian lands,
From sea to sea he sailed and fled,
From land to land he roamed and sped,
Seeking a spot, a place to rest
His bleeding feet and ease his wounded breast.

Thou, beacon to humanity,
Israel, an ever burning bush!
Israel is "the man of sorrow" of history, —
The scapegoat of Nations,
Toiling for his Ideal, the Unity.
It is his blessing and his curse.
Like the Raven he sped to and fro,
Scanning the floods from the heights,
In the valley the watery waste
Claiming tolls, delinquent souls.
Go where he will'd some Haman he met
Barring his way with envy and hate,
Or an Amalek planning to hinder
His path to the land of promise and hope.
At noon time, and quiet hours of night;
His fervent soul crying; "Peace, peace, I plead,"

Then came the comforting, quieting words,
"I will pour my spirit upon thy seed."

Israel's dream of the coming day,
When strife would cease,
When Justice and Truth would guide all men,
Lingered and faded from the horizon; —
Hydra-headed monsters of rapine
Appeared in the darkness of the night,
With torch and sword burning and slaying; —
The brutal force of man let loose,
Anarchy, chaos, Hell all unleashed
From the banks of the Don to the Rhine —
Out of the din the Dreamer came forth,
Blowing the Trumpet!
Be patient, God neither slumbers nor sleeps!

He dreamt he saw a curtain rising,
Revealing a mansion of goodly size
Being built upon the Mountain top —
Of men going thence to learn the truth,
From the golden words of Law and Love
Woofed into a canopy of Peace.
"For the law shall go forth from Zion,
And the word of God from Jerus'lem"
Then shall be sounded in trumpet tones,
The world redeemed!!

WHAT OF TOMORROW?

From printed page and living stage,
    From dell and hill, in voices shrill,
From bloody rage, where battles wage,
    The words still hold, "thou shalt not kill."

From senseless wars by gory Mars,
   From doleful moans and sickening groans,
From painful scars and weeping stars,
   The cry of want appeals to stones.

From ruins of art with pungent smart,
   From reckless waste and brutish haste,
From soulless mart and mourning heart,
   The call for Love is met with Hate.

What of the phase of coming days?
   Will its path of needs be strewn with weeds?
Will want disgrace the coming race,
   With cry unheard when Justice pleads?

ALL IS BENIGN

Though lightnings flash,
And thunders crash,
   And clouds above us roll;
Why should we cry
If dark the sky,
   They do not sear the soul.

Mountains may glow,
Rivers o'erflow,
   'Tis a wondrous plan divine; —
I am quite sure,
Truth will endure,
   For I feel all is benign.

The earth may pall,
And forms may fall,
   And things dear pass away!

Yet all do live
Their worth to give
  And change gloom into day.

Our lives will gain
Through woe and pain,
  Grow fuller by the strife,
So will the soul
Of life's great whole
  Make paths to higher life.

JUSTICE —

I am the Alchemist of the Universe!
  Throughout the ages, I with my sister *Love*
  watched the trend and destiny of Man —
  I was weak and powerless
  in the beginning, when man was so close to
  the beast of the field that his
  ferocity drowned my pleading words.

Centuries of suffering, of distress
  over the world, fills me with anguish;
  my voice though clear and resonant fell upon dull
  dead ears.

I must not tire, I must not fail,
  when the need of me is so great; doubt
  and fear shall not restrain me in my
  effort to open the eyes of men.

LOVE —

Through the ages of travail,
    when the only sound of music was the lullaby
    of the mother to her first born, I listened
    with rapture! Since that day I have never lost hope.

Now *Justice,* my elder brother, is on bended
    knee to me, he implores and pleads my aid,
    I cannot fail him, my voice, though feeble, must respond
    to the call of the hour; I must o'ercome
    the hatred of *Mankind.*

Love shall rule the *World.*

JUSTICE AND LOVE

It is our mission to banish Hatred,
    Injustice and Selfishness in the
    Heart of nations; to banish all misery,
    to bridge the chasm of bigotry and creed and race.

We stand on the heights, we
    see the mists of woe, dissolve —
    and out of all, the soul of man shall
    come purified, cleansed and redeemed.

A VISION AND A HOPE

Ye Monuments of human power and pride!
Ye Pyramids and tombs and structures vain!
In your Art's triumphs, endless toil and strain,
Have vanquished nature and her power defied; —

Ye temples whose vast ruins still abide!
And thou Temple of Judah's checkered reign,
Where Psalmists sang and Prophets warn'd in vain, —
Where Romans shouted while their victims died; —
Time's magic will renew thy high estate,
And bring thy suffering peoples slow relief
To ease and sooth their age-long grief.
Justice and Peace will come to the old state,
Have faith, abiding hope and wait!

VISIONS

I dreamt that all the earth and sea,
   Sunny bowers and coral caves
Were mine; and that my soul was free
   To cleave the air, to sail the waves.
I dreamt! But then a stifled moan
Disturbed that dream — I was alone.

I dreamt that every rare delight
   Of running brooks and trees and flowers,
Hung round my soul's far wand'ring flight;
   I dreamt of years, of days, of hours; —
Time tells me how all these have flown;
I mark the flight, — I am alone.

I dreamt of slums and prison's cells,
   Of toiling slaves in mines and mills,
Drinking from polluted wells,
   Quafing from the brew of stills,
The seed of sin and sorrow sown; —
I may not linger here alone.

I dreamt of men, stalwart and strong;
   Of women chaste and free;

Of children blithe, evoking song,
    Of sunshine full, all guilelessly,
Endowed with joy and hearts bestrown
With blessings born of love alone.

I dreamt of the right of the untrammeled sea,
    Of the earth's open ports and marts;
I dreamt of speech and mind set free,
    Glowing science and its fostering arts;
The aftermath of cruel strife,
The coming dawn of higher life.

I heard the knell of Kingly might,
    The passing of the Lord and Czar;
I dreamt of love; the rule of Right;
    The reign of Peace; the death of War;
This is the day the Lord has made,
Let us be glad, — and unafraid.

EMMA AND LOVE

BY THEIR HANDS WILL YOU
KNOW THEM

I know two women; — the younger is quite fair,
Eyes of liquid blue, hands like ope'ning lilies;
Upon her finger there is a golden ring
With tiny chainlets that bind it to her wrist;
Chains forming a web around her shapely hand,
Nails like ocean shells, clear pinky shells, through which
Rosey tides of blood rise and fall with rhythmic beats.
The moons in her nails are like translucent pearls,
And around them runs a rim of coral pink;
Her hands are perfumed with odor of lily buds,
And you half suspect to see bees buzzing by.

The other woman's hands are not quite so fair,
Down one finger of the tired, worn left hand
Run many needle pricks, callus'd, roughen'd and brown —
She says there are so many holes and rends to mend,
Calls of dishpan tasks, of torn hose and baby's cry
Seem to fill the days from early dawn to dusk.
She will not complain, so long as all is well —
She has just one ring, a batter'd golden band,
That loosely rests on the dried and shrunken flesh,
As a pledge of faith during the trying years,
And a talisman for the coming morrow.

I know two women, one has such hands, upon
Which bees might alight, come in search of honey —
The other has hands that builded roadways, which
Lead and promise to reach the Infinite.

CUPID

A gay vagabond is Love, with a wing,
  Light as gossamer, he rests on a sunbeam,
Or glows in summer mists, he haunts the Spring;
  Gay in the rippling of the sunbright stream.
  In color he rivals the rainbow's gleam; —
He is a truant, 'mid lisping leaves,
  A gay gallant where the young flowers team; —
A garland for his fairy mate he weaves.

How passing strange, he climbs the awful steep
  To bask for a while in the sun-lit heights,
Goes down for treasures in the coral's deep,
  Disputes the reign of the tempest brooding night,
  Quenches the fires of War. Nor famine's blight,
Nor hot Equator's flush, nor Arctic cold
  Can stay him in his Universal might;
A paradox, he is gentle, he is bold.

He is capricious; often seizing hearts
  That least suspect him, and as often he
Doth sport most gaily, whence in sudden starts, —
  Hair breadth escapes, and bouts in which he
  Not always seems most wise in chastity —
In passionate momentary wanderings
  And long consistent quiet, never free,
Yet welcome spirit where he rests his wings.

If now in the bright sensation of an hour
  He flits from scene to scene in gorgeous hues;
Soon o'er his bloom, sweet tasks, his wings will lower
  And he with lurking hopes content, will choose
  To taste the sweets, and then in silence muse,

Perhaps to fail, or blossom with success; —
   His task is sweet, he cannot be refused;
Though often blind, his mission is to bless.

TO THE MEMORY OF HER
WHO WAS OF ME A PART

Years in which you were so much a part:
Fraught with longing hopes and loving tears,
Gleams of sunlight streaming through the years —
Are but jewels of your tender heart.
Dear lips, speaking kind words whene'er I fell,
Soft hands, stroking my fevered brow, —
Swift feet coming softly to my aid; and now,
Memories of years their stories tell.
No time can, from my mind, your love efface; —
Those sweet days, wherein you kissed to bless;
The thoughts that came, could I express
Would all the grief of our parting made, erase.
Nor time nor space take heed of years —
Before me, you I see, in mind and heart,
Through years in which you were so much a part; —
Today I bring you tribute, — *tears.*

OUR BETROTHAL
[*May 1st, 1867*]

As now the lights are quenched, the night is still and clear;
There comes to me sweet memories of many a vanished
                                                year.
The Day and the Year around me flit, like clouds in the sky;
Roseate was our outlook then, our pulses beating high.

Ah! days of our wedded life, gaining strength from year to
year,
In which we made the "milk way" a starry bridge of cheer.
As the days and years were passing, there came a likely
band,
That helped to span the sea of space, as we walked hand in
hand.

MARCH FOURTH
1896–1916

A score of years, of smiles and tears,
    Of light and shade, of bloom and blight,
Of faith and love beyond the spheres,
    Of help and hope in darkest night.

Flowers you loved are just as bright,
    And yet, at times they seem to crave
Such love and care to guide them right
    As in those years of life you gave.

The for-get-me-not is still kept green,
    Where planted by your loving care; —
Yea, in my heart it may be seen
    Shielded from stress and curious glare.

The months and years make up the score;
    The days grow shorter, nearing West,
The hours fly swifter than of yore;
    Tho' nights are long, with broken rest.

I often see you in a dream,
    As on that day of May you gave

Your heart to me to sail Life's stream. —
   Your smile again I crave.

Or on that fond September day,
   When we two sang the nuptial psalm,
Forty-nine years — remember pray,
   To be as one through storm and calm.

Today here I and loved ones meet,
   To lift a chant above your grave,
To keep alive your love so sweet,
   And to praise God for what He gave.

MUSINGS

To my ears there comes not the sound of words,
Nor children's sweet laughter or song of birds,
When to church on Sabbath day I repair,
To offer there, a heartfelt praise and prayer.
Faint are the words of God and sacred strains,
To me in that abode, calm silence reigns;
Dim are the sacred songs that sweep the lute;
Naught but their echoes float into my solitude;
And memory brings again those sweetest lays,
Sung by my faithful mate in bygone days.

TOMORROW

When I am dead, Beloved, when I am dead,
And all the mortal flesh of me is dust,
And now the tale of all my little hour is thrust
Entirely from the minds of men and fled,
I like to think of all those things I love —

Of May's betrothal, of September's reign,
These still recur and comfort me again,
And send their fragrance to me from above;
Of days that made us one, of the scent
Of Autumn's flowers that bloom along life's stream,
Will be to me an earthly sacrament!
To light and sanctify my age-long dream!
I would believe, that some time I shall hear
A whisper of the voice, to me most dear.

YESTERDAY AND TODAY
In Memoriam of the Twenty-fifth Anniversary of My Wife's Death
Born July 9, 1838; Died March 4, 1896

On the summit of years fourscore, —
    With the shadows of life behind,
Laden with promise held in store
    Of memories lasting and kind;
There looms one face serene and bright
    That held me bound in silken cords;
In brightest day and darkest night
    Encouraged me with cheering words.

Through lonely hours and weary miles,
    Bereft of her these many years;
She comes to me with loving smiles,
    In my mourning and flowing tears.
This day, five and twenty years ago,
    Sore and weary she went to sleep;
Left me alone my bark to row
    In storm and breakers of the deep.

When doubt and dread blinded my sight,
    When faith and hope shrouded my heart,

There came to me in darkest night
    From spirit land, a guiding chart; —
Oft in my dreams she comes to me,
    Her face lit up with sweetest smile,
With loving words reminding me
    Of my duties for yet a while.

Many burdens she laid on me,
    Which I carried the best I could,
Laden with years my heart is free,
    Do what I can, the best I would.
Alas, there is so much undone,
    Awaiting before I rest,
Mindful I am, much like the Sun
    I'm facing, towards the West.

Of the many gifts transcending
    She brought and gave the best,
Her heart forever tending
    With cheer and love to test.
The best example she set for all,
    So humble and modest was she,
Alert to heed the midnight call
    With real efficiency.

When my weakening eyes shall close
    In the last long dreamless sleep,
When my ailments shall find repose
    Where grief and sorrow cease to weep.
When I have stemmed each stormy wave
    Of life, from its temptations free,
I feel assured, beyond the grave,
    Thou'lt ope Heav'n's gate for me.

If thoughts on earth may reach thy state,
    Let this message assurance give,

That thy offsprings may emulate
    Your teachings in the lives they live.
Respectful of the young and old
    Which thou hast fostered in their youth,
A legacy more dear than gold
    And one enduring as the truth.

I cannot reach my life's ideal,
    Of which I dreamed these many years,
It lies ahead; I sense and feel
    A life to come in other spheres,
Where souls await to meet again,
    Complete the task unfinished here,
Where spirit now released from pain,
    Can make its claim, a title clear.

Why should we paint, mighty King Death,
    In such a terrible array?
A spectre form, a grizzly [sic] thing,
    Before whose look all shrink away?
A dark monster of vengeance sent
    To blight, to conquer and destroy,
God's fierce and deadly instrument,
    Blasting all our buds of Joy?

As lightnings purge the tainted air,
    Leaving no trace of aught unclean,
So Death, perhaps, may bring to bear
    The ripening fruit to eyes unseen.
So seeming ills may cleanse our life,
    Throw off the dross we gather here,
The Mystic way to end all strife; —
    If so, the price is not too dear.

When that day comes, as soon it will,
   When my journey shall close and end,
And life's stream flow over the hill
   That sought to help and strove to mend
The broken ties 'tween man and man,
   I hope to feel with calm content
My efforts here were not in vain
   Though short and weak the instrument.

A DREAM AND ITS MESSAGE

What mean you by this weeping
   To break my very heart?
We are both in God's keeping,
   And therefore cannot part.

Though our lives have been severed,
   We still in heart are one,
Many storms we have weathered,
   Their shadows scarcely gone.

Though clouds still surround you —
   Is not life an open sea?
Lift up your eyes and seek the way,
   That leads from you to me.

I was so ill and weary,
   Surely you should not frown,
In having gone before you,
   To lay my burdens down.

Then weep not, weep not, darling,
   God wipes away all tears,
'Tis only yet a little while,
   Though you may call it years.

MIDNIGHT MUSINGS

Musing oft in midnight hours,
   Of things long since past and gone,
Not a heart to beat responsive
   To the throbbing of my own.
The past often comes before me,
   In a solemn slow review
Days of gladness, days of sorrow,
   In a picture, I renew.

Oft the image of my dear one,
   Angel of my youth appears,
Beautiful she stands before me,
   After lapse of many years,
Then again her form approaching,
   Her dear lips are pressed to mine,
Her dark eyes in mine upgazing,
   With a trust and love divine.

AN INVOCATION

Bring back the time when glad desire ran free,
With bit and rein too loose to curb his flight.
The tears and flames that in one breast unite,
If thou art feign once more to conquer me.

Bring back those journeys made so toilsomely, —
So toilsome slow to him whose hairs are white,
Give back the buried face, once angel-bright,
Garbed during all her days with modesty.

O Love, an old man finds it hard to chase
Thy flying pinions; — thou hast left thy nest,

Nor is my heart as light as heretofore,
Put thy gold arrows to the string once more; —

Then if Death hear my prayers and grant me grace,
I'll meet thy dear familiar presence, face to face.

GRIEF AND DEATH

MEDITATION

There is a pensive craving known to men
By many names, though one alone befits
Its mystery, its beauty and its power;
It is not fear, 'tis not the doubting dread
That fails to grasp the future, nor the dark
Despondency that hangs upon the past;
Nor that which fears itself, or slowly feeds
Like a canker worm, until the heart decay.
Grief may sublimate itself, pluck the sting
From out its breast, and muse until it seems
Ethereal, starry, speculative, wise;
And then it is, that meditation comes
To charm our grief, like the "gray morning stills
The tempest oft" and from its inner self
Brings forth a light divine!

DEATH

I am the key that parts the gates of Fame,
I am the cloak that covers cowering shame!
I am the goal that limits every race,
I am the storm-tossed spirit's resting place —
The messenger of sure and swift relief!
Received with wailings, tears and speechless grief,
The friend of those that have no friend but me!
I break all chains and set all captives free —
I am the cloud that shrouds the course you've run!
An instant veil upon the work you've done!
I am the brooding hush that follows strife,
The waking from a dream that man calls life.

DUST TO DUST

All things around us preach of death, yet mirth
Swells the vain heart, darts from careless eye,
As if it were created ne'er to die,
And have an everlasting home on earth —

All things around us teach of death; the leaves
Drop from the forest; so die all the flowers,
So shortens day, its sunlight hours on hours:
And o'er bleak naked fields the wild wind grieves —

All things preach of death; we are born, for dying,
We are but waves along life's ocean driven;
Time is to us a brief probation given
To spend each hour and day, in wisely trying —

To fit us for what is to be,
For that great end, we call Eternity.

THE SPEED DEMON

The dazzling sunshine dances in the street,
        Along the highways light and shadows play,
        And little children come to greet the day,
And join the festal dance with nimble feet,
When lo! around the curve comes demon fleet, —
        A car! and since no mortal life indeed
        Can cope with cruel power, — mad for speed, —
A little child lies dead upon the street.

O Man! is Traffic's mood but to destroy?
        Is Commerce of such price, that it should pay
        No heed to little children at their play?

Defiant of life's dearest earthly joy?
    If speed indeed must be so senseless wild,
    Kill doting age, but you might spare the child.

ON SEEING A SKELETON
(*In a dream*)

What was thy station, high or low,
  Upon the scroll of fame?
And yet it little recks to know,
  From where or whence ye came.

Go now and tell the conqueror,
  No longer may he tread
And drive his scythed car along,
  Upon the martyred dead.
That soon shall fall his tottering throne
That soon his scepter shall be gone!

Tell all, the king upon his throne,
  The slave on cringing knee,
The monarch proud, the captive prone,
  The bondsman and the free;
Tell them that all must come to this,
These are the only vestiges
Of all mortality;
A nameless clod, a lifeless clay,
Spurned by each careless foot away.

GOALS

There is a threnody in words unspoken,
And tears unseen and sighs unheard,

May be but echoes of a heart that's broken.
Does death end all in endless sleep?
Is life a game and we the pawn?
And is the symphony of Spheres
A tolling dirge we hear at Dawn?
Where is our goal?
We come to life without our ken,
And we go out against our will,
We act our part, as best we can,
We are a sigh, a sob, a thrill.
We leave a likely house of life,
To enter one with brighter light,
And we shall find our sacred goal
When we have reached the Infinite.

WHY TEARS?

I want no sad lamenting tears
   When I set sail to sea,
No stifled cries or heaving sighs
   To speed me to eternity:

No crepe or dreary garments worn
   To make my going sad,
But have them white: Something bright:
   Discard old custom's fad.

I want no dirge sung for me
   When I am gone away,
Play something grand, by loving hands
   To make a good glad day.

And let no words be said for me
   That, "He is dead and gone"

But only say, "He left today,
    He's journeyed out and on."

And if some parting tears are shed,
    Just make them all of joy.
Have no regret, be glad we met,
    And say, "Good ship, Ahoy."

October 21, 1922.

THE PASSING

We stand beside the open grave,
We look and ask is this the end?
Will our hopes and plans to ashes turn
Does the path of right end in gloom?

Does the mountlet that holds our dust,
Does the bier of a loving soul,
Sever the tie and sacred trust,
When the body is stiff and cold?

Does death end all? There comes a voice
Gested in our intuition
That tells us that discords of life,
Are but broken chords of harmony!

    That we, young and old, rich and poor, are deathless,
that we'll meet again, that this life is the vestibule, of the
Temple beyond the skies.

    'Tis said, Death loves a shining mark, if so, his arrow
flew with full force, when it came to Laurens Block.

Alas! his life was all too short, reckoning as we do, in days, months and years; yet when we consider the achievements; four score years, could do no more.

A devoted husband and father; a loving son and brother, a man who kept alive the sense and touch of kinship by unselfish thought and deed.

Dead; no; his spirit remains and hovers in the hearts of those he loved and among those he toiled. He was an inspiration to higher ideals to his co-workers. He laid a foundation solid and deep, that makes for the brotherhood of man.

I almost envy the part he played in the drama of life — he broke bread with those hungered, he gave of his spirit to them that were broken, and strength to them that were weak; he lived.

"A noble life, a simple faith,
    An open heart and hand.
These are the lovely litanies
    Which all men understand."

Thy spirit guides beloved son,
    "I cease from my song to thee."

November 11, 1920.

LIFE, SEASONS, AND NATURE

MYSTERIES

O Earth! thou hast not any wind that blows
Which is not music; every weed of thine,
Pressed rightly, flows with aromatic wine;
And every humble hedgerow flower that grows,
And every little brown birdling that sings,
Hath something greater than itself, and bears
A living word to all the living things;
All shapes and sounds have something which is not
Of them. A spirit broods amid the grass; —
Deep outlines of the everlasting Thought
Lie in the fleeting shadows as they pass.
The touch of Eternal mystery thrills
The fringes of the sunset and the hills.
Sometimes (we know not why nor whence) —
The chirping of the swallows, 'neath the eaves,
The shimmer of the light among the leaves,
Will strike up in the thick roof of our sense,
And show us things which sage and poet saw.
Something doth stir
Like organ fugues within us,
And doth awe our feelings into listening,
And confer burdens of Being on us;
And we ache with weights of mysteries;
And our ears hear voices from the Infinite,
That take the hushed soul captive.

TIME

Father Time has lately shown many moods; —
The riotous colors of Autumn are gone,
The peaceful monotones of Winter crown
With frost the mountain range, valley and woods.

Time; a wonderful alchemist art thou —
The oldest year of the world dead and gone,
While the youngest comes without a frown,
Bearing tidings of cheer upon his brow —
The old and the new met and came on time
Alike heedless of centuries and cycles
Of titanic struggles and frivolous trifles
Straining history's pages in every clime;
Is Time Life's continuity,
Or a symbol of Eternity?

ECHOES

We the miracle born of sound,
  Where the sweetest spots are found,
  Over sea, over land,
  An invisible band.
Finding sport on every ground,
  We love not the plain,
  Nor the sky bound main;
Nor delight in either to reign;
  But enraptured we dwell
  In the wood or the dell,
In shady moor, or rocking shore,
Romping merrily o'er and o'er.

In a rock upon the shore,
Oft we mock the ocean's roar,
Or on green hillsides at dawn,
Carol to the huntsman's horn!
Or at evening in the vale
Listen to the shepherd's tale;
On feet of air we glide along,
Or warble to a tuneful song,

Where magic tones of music dwell
  We lurk and answer,
   Swell for swell;
Half the charm that music knows,
To the Echo's voice she owes.

THE MASTER WEAVER

The shuttles of the sun fly fast,
  Between a warp of boughs;
'Tis the Master Weaver at his work,
  Fulfilling all his vows.

In Spring his loom is full of bloom,
  In Summer full of green;
But when the crickets wake and sing,
  His glowing waves are seen.

With royal purple, red and gold,
  With brown and silver gray,
He decks each weed, and bush and fold,
  Then wanders far away.

He fares into a realm of snow,
  To paint more subtle beams;
On wintry nights, his Northern Lights
  Are shuttles weaving dreams.

PATIENCE AND WILL

How patiently the birds await the Spring,
How constantly the corols toil;

How long the spider crouches for his spoil.
With endless patience does the wild fowl wing.

How calmly flake by flake the great drift forms —
How steadfastly the camel bears his draught!
How slowly is matured each potent thought,
How lofty spirits weather adverse storms.

This is the test of mighty souls and true!
To have to suffer much and falter not;
By these great ends designed, all things are wrought.
Aspiring Soul! make it thy glory too!

DAY

If life has naught for us beyond this earth;
 A few brief cheering years, then starless night;
 If that which stirs our hearts, that inner light,
Is but a hope, which in our fear has birth;
 If only these, we have; — bright childhood's dreams,
Youth's forward urge, strong manhood's doughty deeds,
The sweet old age which loving memory feeds,
 These were enough, though false all future gleams.
To view one dawn is worth a lifetime's price;
 To greet one Spring, that will old griefs repay;
 To trust one friend, makes glad the Pilgrim's way.
Though night come fast, those with our heart suffice, —
 Give me belief and hope beyond the night,
 Beyond the ended day, unending light.

NIGHT

O Blessed Twilight, come and bring me balm,
For eyes grown weary of the garrish [sic] day,

Come with thy soft slow steps, thy garments gray,
Thy veiling shadows bearing in thy palm
The poppy seeds of slumber, deep and calm.
Come with the patient stars, whose far off ray
Drives the thought of the fevered mind away;
Thy whispers sweeter than a chanted psalm.
O blessed darkness, day indeed is fair,
So is quiet dear, when summer days are gone,
And thy night lamps one by one come by!
And so is rest sweet, and surcease from care;
The sleeping trees and hush of evening song,
And all the unmeasured silence of the sky.

A DREAM

If one who looks upon a glorious day
Expiring on the threshold of the West, —
Must breathe a thoughtful wish
That here he stay, —
And feel within him dying, unexpressed
The seer-voiced longing of the heart's unrest;
May we not trust,
That in the "evermore,"
A friendlier clime awaits the pensive breast?

Must it fore'er remain, that all the earth
Shall be a field of barrenness?
A gloomy waste of hollow sounds?
Must fruitless Nature see the season's end,
And sunless days the last?
Must Time in silence view the broken urn,
Or sit and brood upon an empty past?

If conscious life about the earth might stroll,
A child of reason still; —

It then were sweet to think
Of a Republic of the Soul
Where communes of the spirits meet
To walk the earth they've known
With steadfast feet.

If then this be,
How good this pleasing dream;
When Life brought light to darkest mine
And leads the humblest to her lone wood-stream
To seek a haven,
'Neath her leafy shrine
In pathos deep —
In tenderness divine.

A SONG OF PRAISE AND FAITH

O Blessed April! Month of showers,
The month that gave me light of day, —
Full four-score years ago, — and now I pray
That April rains will bring me flowers
Of many hues for all my hours; —
Strengthen my heart to hold at bay
Shadowing doubts, and thoughts of clay,
I start my journey with Faith ahead,
My anchor is raised, my sails are spread.

POEMS ON VARIOUS SUBJECTS

YOUTH

Youth is not a time of life; it is a state of mind; it is not a matter of rosy cheeks, red lips and supple knees; it is a matter of the will, a quality of the imagination, a vigor of the emotions; it is the freshness of the deep springs of life.

Youth means a temperamental predominance of courage over timidity of the appetite, for adventure over the love of ease. This often exists in a man of sixty more than a boy of twenty. Nobody grows old merely by a number of years. We grow old by deserting our ideals.

Years may wrinkle the skin, but to give up enthusiasm wrinkles the soul. Worry, fear, self-distrust bows the heart and turns the spirit back to dust.

Whether sixty or sixteen, there is in every human being's heart the lure of wonder, the unfailing child-like appetite of what's next, and the joy of the game of living. In the center of your heart and my heart there is a wireless station; so long as it receives messages of beauty, hope, cheer, courage and power from men and from the Infinite, so long are you young.

When the aerials are down, and your spirit is covered with snows of cynicism and the ice of pessimism, then you are grown old, even at twenty, but as long as your aerials are up, to catch the waves of optimism, there is hope you may die young at eighty.

WHAT'S YOUR HURRY?

Slack up, brother, what's your hurry,
That so recklessly you scurry,

With your elbows crowding sideways
And your eyes fixed straight ahead?
Is a minute's time so precious,
That you need be so ungracious,
And go tramping on your fellows,
As on the way you speed?

Can't you spare a nod of greeting,
Pass the time of day in meeting,
Swap a joke or smile a little
When a neighbor comes along?
Is the dollar so enticing —
Is success so all-sufficing
That you can't devote a second
To a brother in the throng?

Do you know your destination?
It's a quiet little station,
Where ambition never troubles
And the dollar jingles not; —
Where riches are not enduring,
Where your note has passed maturing,
And the richest man's possession
Is a little grassy spot.

Why be over keen in speeding,
On a trail so surely leading
To that lonely little city, where
We all must land at last?
Slack up, brother! What's your hurry,
That so recklessly you scurry?
You may lead a slow procession
E'er another year is past.

Lincoln Newfield, circa 1915. (Photograph courtesy of Mayer U. Newfield.)

UNTITLED

I see and ask, is it fact or fancy,
A trick of some playful necromancy,
That leads him to bed in folding pillow,
The sky for canopy, the rock for pillow?

Like a bud in springtime, lovely and fair,
Kissed by sunlight and the morning air?
Listening to a song or story half told,
Or of visions sensed on fields of gold?

[This poem was written by Ullman in 1915 in response to seeing
the photograph of his grandson Lincoln seeking warmth from a
large rock near the cold waters where he had been swimming
near Petoskey, Michigan. Lincoln was four years old at the time
of the photograph.]

MY PIPE

With rubber stem, with bowl of brier,
Largely serving my desire,
Many secrets thou dost bear
Within thy brownish bosom rare.

My fond hopes and dreams thou knowest,
Of the highest, of the lowest;
Ever soothing, ever pleasing,
Never taunting, never teasing.

Intimate, yea, most familiar,
Dearer far than gold or silver,
Jolly Pal, — yea, closest friend,
Let me woo thee to the end.

YOU AND I

If I knew you and you knew me,
If both of us could clearly see,
And with an inner light divine
The longings of your heart and mine,
I'm sure that we would differ less,
We'd clasp our hands in friendliness,
Our thoughts would surely then agree,
If I knew you and you knew me.

DUTY

Hark! I hear shrill voices speaking,
   In the quiet hours of night,
Listen, you may hear them calling
   In the distress of their plight.

Calling, pleading, go and help them;
   Will you fail them, you who know?
You who've learned the way of duty;
   You who know the way to go.

If you were lost within the marshes,
   Without compass, guide, or light,
Could you find your way unaided;
   Would you know which way was right?
You must let the light within you
   Shine for others gone astray,
And by aiding and directing
   Help them find a better way.

IT MATTERS NOT

It matters not if heads be white,
   If your heart and thought be young,
If in your soul there be a light
   And a song upon your tongue.

GROWING APACE

When the morning calls me early,
         And the day
Seems to find me somewhat churly
         With the way;
Loosing some of its old charm,
Is there reason for alarm?
         When I crave more time for leisure
Caring less and less for gold,
         Is it just the way it happens,
Or is it, I am growing old?

Well, I don't intend to worry,
    If it's true,
I shall not lament and hurry
    Though eighty-two,
I shall greet each new born day,
In the same old patient way,
    I will meet my round of duties
As the days to me are doled,
    Thankful, cheerful, always hopeful,
Though perhaps, I'm growing old.

WEAVING

I weave wearing cares into dreams,
    I cast away blinding dross,
I bring forth the light that gleams,
    And put aside tinsel and gloss.

I weave straying leaves into forests,
    And dew-drops into seas,
I braid loose grass into bowers
    And weeds transform into flowers.

I sense the current of the heart,
    The smile that gleams in the eye,
And with the mists that rise and fall,
    Drape white clouds in the sky.

VALENTINES ON LIFE'S HIGHWAYS

I would not ask for a thornless life,
    From every sorrow free,
Or for a constant sunshine,
    Or for a summer's sea.

For as the verdure of the earth,
    Would wither and decay,
Beneath a constant sunshine
    Or a perpetual day;

So the deep chamber of the heart,
    Throughout the years,
Would cease to yield the buds of hope,
    If watered not by tears,

There's much that lies within the reach,
    Of life in every field;
Which if intelligently tilled,
    Will a rich harvest yield.

A TRIED REMEDY

When you arise in the morning,
    To start the coming day,
Try this recipe for happiness,
    I am sure that it will pay.

First of all begin with a smile,
    That starts from your mouth and eyes,
Then offer a cheery good morning,
    'Twill make you happy and wise.
A kind word will flavor your greeting,
    A caress will sweeten the day,
A helpful deed will lighten
    The gloom that lurks by the way!
Soft words will brighten the outlook
    With a clear and rosy hue,
A laugh will lessen the shadows
    That seek to dishearten you.

Come, follow this recipe closely,
    It's simple and easy, I say,
And you will reap richly your sowing,
    And be sure of a brighter day.

Come now, try a bit of laughter,
    A hand shake and a smile,
You'll need little more hereafter,
    If you try this once in a while.

SMILE

Smile! 'Tis a phase of beauty,
    Smile! 'Tis a stamp of art;
Smile! 'Tis a story all can read —
    It is current on every mart.

Smile! 'Tis a balm for care;
    'Tis an antidote for woe,
Smile! 'Tis the unspoken prayer,
    And the bond to high and low.

I see it in the lily fair,
    And in the royal rose,
I see it in the violet,
    In every flower that grows.

I see it in the rising sun,
    And in the twilight hour;
I see it in the starlit night
    And in the snow and shower.

I see it in the ocean wave;
    And in the ambient air,

I see it in the mountain spring,
    I see it everywhere.

I hear it in the cricket's chirp
    And in the robin's lay,
I hear it in the thrush's song,
    I hear it night and day.

Smile! 'Tis a staff to the lame,
    Smile! 'Tis an eye to the blind,
Smile! 'Tis in the timely word
    Voiced to the troubled mind.

A smile is on the outer face,
    Born of the inner heart.
Here Hope and Faith each other meet,
    Here Truth and Love play a part.

TELL ME

Why do smiles sometimes repel us,
    Bright eyes turn our feelings cold?
What is that which comes to tell us
    All that glitters is not gold?
Then comes a figure, plain or striking,
    With an aim we cannot shun,
Prompts our liking or disliking,
    E'er acquaintance is begun.

Is it instinct or some spirit
    Which protects us and controls
Every impulse we inherit,
    By some sympathy of souls?

Is it instinct, is it feeling,
    Or some freak or trick of chance?
Which our liking or disliking
    Revealeth in a single glance?

Tell me by what means or teaching
    Our impressions first are led
Into liking or disliking,
    Oft before a word is said.
Ah, I ask can no one tell me,
    No one show sufficient cause,
If our liking or disliking
    Have their own distinctive laws?

A LAY OF CHEER

It isn't the people you know,
    Though they're likely a very good sort;
It isn't the jewels you show,
    No matter how much you're a sport.
It isn't the gambling you do,
    E'en though you are likely to win,
It's the way that your mouth
Turns to north and to south
    That brings a grin,
        The grin,
            Your grin.

It isn't the way that you talk,
    It isn't the thing that you say,
It isn't your manner of walk,
    Or the pleasure you get when you play,
It isn't the knowledge you have,
    Although this is doubtless worth while,

No, it's not your looks,
Or the things found in books,
  That brings a smile,
      The smile,
          Your smile.

For a grin and a smile means a laugh,
  And a laugh is the most cheerful thing,
That one can use, for a bit of the blues,
  To stave off the pain and dull sting.
So if others are gloomy and sad,
  And inclined to make mischief and chaff,
Just pull down your vest,
And puff out your chest,
  And give them a laugh,
      The laugh,
          Your laugh.

I AM MERRY WHEN I MAY

O yes, I'm happy when I can,
  I'm merry when I may,
For Life's at most a narrow span;
  At best a summer day.
If Care could make a sunbeam wear
  A brighter, warmer hue,
The evening star shine out more fair,
  And the sky look more blue,
Then I might be a graver man; —
  Since this is not the way,
Therefore I'm happy when I can
  And merry when I may.

If want could make me see the loss,
  Perchance I would be glad.

If mourning be the sage's dress,
  My garb would then be sad.
They say that angels' robes are white,
  And the saints wear a smile,
That Virtue wears a robe of light,
  And Vice a brow of guile.
As laughter is not under ban,
  Nor gladness clad in gray;
Therefore I'm happy when I can
  And merry when I may.

I've seen a preacher dance a reel,
  A sinner fast and pray,
A knave on top of fortune's wheel,
  And a good man cast away.
The grave ones oft the wine do quaff,
  Act gayly as a goat,
But I never heard a hearty laugh
  From out a villain's throat.
And I never knew a cheerful man,
  Sing a long mournful lay,
Therefore I'm happy when I can
  And merry when I may.

Notes

1. "Youth": A Philosophy, a Bridge

1. Len Boselovic, "Rhyme and reason at National Steel provided by poem," *The Pittsburgh Press*, 1 July 1990, D 15.

2. "How to Stay Young" document, MacArthur Papers, MacArthur Memorial, Norfolk, Virginia (hereinafter MacArthur Papers). The inscription reads, "To General and Mrs. Douglas McArthur [*sic*] Best Wishes of John W. Lewis, Jr., 4-11-1942"; "How to Stay Young," *This Week*, 30 September 1945, in Mayer U. Newfield Papers, private collection, Birmingham, Alabama, (hereinafter MUN Papers); telephone conversation with Edward J. Boone, Jr., archivist, MacArthur Memorial, 10 January 1990. No information on the identity of Lewis has been discovered despite the best efforts of the author, officials of the MacArthur Memorial, and Munehisa Sakuyama (Sakuyama to John M. Leeds, Jr., 13 February 1986, MacArthur Papers). *Reader's Digest* possesses a letter from Lewis that they declined to share with the author because of privacy concerns. The letter suggests that Lewis liberally gave away copies of the unattributed version of Ullman's poem. Perhaps Lewis's family will come forward, as Ullman's did, to provide identifying information. Interestingly, two years after Palmer's encounter, MacArthur's aide-de-camp, Lawrence E. Bunker, responded to an inquiry about the work by saying that General MacArthur "did not recall" where he first ran across the poem (Bunker to Mrs. Tetsuko K. Suzuki, 29 November 1947, MacArthur Papers).

3. Interview with Mayer U. Newfield, Birmingham, Alabama, 9 August 1989; Osamu Uno, letter to author, 23 February 1990. [Samuel Ullman], *From the Summit of Years, Four Score* (Los Angeles: Fred S. Lang Company Publishers, 1922).

4. Robert H. Alexander, Director of the MacArthur Memorial, to Research Division, Birmingham Public Library, 20 August 1973; Robert H. Alexander to Carol Coon, Reference Librarian, San Francisco Public Library, 31 July 1975, MacArthur Papers (Copies in possession of author); Tatsuro Ishida, letter to author, 8 March 1990; Munehisa Sakuyama, letter to author, 23 February 1990; Uno to author.

5. Edward N. MacConomy, Acting Chief, Library of Congress Reference ' Department, to Librarian, MacArthur Memorial, 2 March 1973, MacArthur Papers; Whitman Daniels, Director of Public Relations, Associated Industries of New York State, to General Douglas MacArthur, 25 February 1952, MacArthur Papers.

6. D. Clayton James, *The Years of MacArthur*, Vol. 3, *Triumph and Disaster, 1945–1964* (Boston: Houghton-Mifflin, 1985), 665–66; "The General's Moment," *Newsweek* 45 (17 February 1955): 22; "As Young as Your Faith," *Time* 65 (7 February 1955): 14; "Notes and Comments," *New Yorker* 30 (5 February 1955): 21–22.

7. George E. Sokolsky, "From A Summit of Years — Four Score," New York *Journal American*, 10 March 1955; "Poem may hold strength for MacArthur," *Birmingham News*, 5 April 1964 (Associated Press article); "Poem penned here inspired MacArthur," *Birmingham News*, 7 April 1964.

8. Senator Kennedy's eulogy can be found in *Vital Speeches of the Day* 34 (1 July 1968): 546–47; Edward Forman, NBC News, New York, letter to author, 23 December 1991.

9. Ishida to author; "A Bridge Called 'The Youth,'" videotape (1987), in possession of author; "Japan," *Forbes* 144 (24 July 1989): 176; Steve Lohr, "Kounosuke Matsushita, Industrialist, Is Dead at 94," *New York Times*, 28 April 1989.

10. Ishida to author; Uno to author; Sakuyama to author. Kansai is the second largest city in Japan. Toyo Boseki employs 30,000 people, according to Japan *Times*, 6 January 1987, MUN Papers.

11. Uno to author; Sakuyama to author; information sheet on *A Poem Titled "Youth": The Phantom Poet, Samuel Ullman* (Tokyo: Sanno Institute of Business Administration, 1986), MUN Papers. As of 1990 over 120,000 copies of this work had been sold in Japan.

12. Jiro Miyazawa, letter to author, 1 June 1992; Jiro Miyazawa,

Youth, translated into English by Thomas K. Mishima (privately printed, n.d.), copy in possession of author.

13. "Youth" videotape; information sheet on Tatsuro Ishida; Mayer Newfield to Mr. and Mrs. Robert Lehman, 29 July 1988, MUN Papers; "A Night When 200 Executives Return to Young Time," *Friday* (Japanese weekly newspaper), 9 October 1987, in MUN Papers; Joe Kiefer, "Ullman poem strikes chord, prompts visit," *Birmingham News,* 27 February 1988; Alec Harvey, "Poem by city education pioneer will be honored by the Japanese," *Birmingham News,* 30 August 1987.

14. "Youth" videotape; Kiefer, "Ullman poem strikes chord." Toppan Moore is a subsidiary of Toppan Printing Company, Limited, which employs 14,000 people in twenty-one plants throughout Japan.

15. Ishida to author; Uno to author; Sakuyama to author. Over 10,000 copies of the Japanese version of *From the Summit of Years, Four Score* had been sold by 1990.

16. Information sheet on Chiyohiko Asano and letters from juveniles, enclosed in letter from Ishida to author.

2. *Old World, New World*

1. Newfield family Bible held by Mrs. Semon U. Newfield, Birmingham, Alabama; Ullman Family Document held by Mrs. Robert (Elaine) Lehman, private collection, Natchez, Mississippi (hereinafter Lehman Papers); Samuel Ullman to Richard Fries, 17 July 1920, Morris Newfield Papers, Department of Archives and Manuscripts, Birmingham Public Library (hereinafter Newfield Papers). Copies in possession of author. Mrs. Newfield is Ullman's granddaughter-in-law; Mrs. Lehman is Ullman's grandniece; Richard Fries was Ullman's nephew-in-law.

2. Newfield Bible; William L. Langer, comp. and ed., *An Encyclopedia of World History* (Boston: Houghton Mifflin, 1972), 678, 715–16; Abram Leon Sachar, *A History of the Jews* (New York: Alfred A. Knopf, 1965), 286; Eli Evans, *The Provincials: A Personal History of Jews in the South* (New York: Atheneum, 1973), 45.

3. Ullman to Fries; Ullman Family Document.

4. Newfield Bible; Richard L. Greaves, Robert Zoller, Philip V. Cannistraro, and Rhoads Murphy, *Civilizations of the World* (New York: Harper and Row, 1990), 739–46; Sachar, *History of the Jews,* 291; Ullman to Fries.

5. Ullman to Fries; Newfield Bible; Leo E. Turitz and Evelyn Turitz, *Jews in Early Mississippi* (Jackson: University Press of Mississippi, 1983), x; Sachar, *History of the Jews,* 304.

6. Katy McCaleb Headley, *Claiborne County, Mississippi: The Promised Land* (Port Gibson, Miss.: Claiborne County Historical Society, 1976), 6; Richard Aubrey McLemore, ed., *A History of Mississippi,* 2 vols. (Hattiesburg: University and College Press of Mississippi, 1973), 1: 256, 527; D. Clayton James, *Antebellum Natchez* (Baton Rouge: Louisiana State University Press, 1968), 190, 227.

7. McLemore, *History of Mississippi,* 1: 393, 424; Temple Gemiluth Chassed, 1859 cash book, pp. 4–5, located in American Jewish Archives, Hebrew Union College, Cincinnati, Ohio; Evans, *The Provincials,* x, 4–6, 72–87. The temple cash book lists both Jacob and Samuel Ullman as charter members.

8. Ullman Family Document; Newfield Bible; Ullman to Fries; genealogy of Ullman family, Lehman Papers.

9. Ullman to Fries; Harris Gaylord Warren, "People and Occupations in Port Gibson, 1860," *Journal of Mississippi History* 10 (April 1948): 107. Ullman never mentioned his father's slaves in his spoken or written memories of his youth, and there are no records of the function Jacob Ullman's slaves played in the family business or home.

10. J. Stoddard Johnston, ed., *Memorial History of Louisville from its First Settlement to the Year 1896,* 2 vols. (Chicago and New York: American Biographical Publishing Company, 1896), 2: 274; *A History of the Jews of Louisville, Ky. Illustrated with Magnificent Half-Tone Cuts of Prominent Jews, Jewesses, Clubs, Temples, etc.* (New Orleans: Jewish Historical History [LA], c. 1900), 13, 16; *Louisville (Ky.) City Directory,* 1861, 337; Joseph Cohen, "Early Louisville Jewish History," *The Chronicler* 8 (May 1920): 3; Herman Landau, *Adath Louisville: The Story of a Jewish Community* (Louisville, Ky.: Herman Landau and Associates, 1981), 22–23.

11. Ullman to Fries.

12. Ibid.; Mark Cowett, *Birmingham's Rabbi: Morris Newfield and Alabama, 1895–1940* (Tuscaloosa: University of Alabama Press, 1986), 27.

13. Ullman to Fries.

14. Dunbar Rowland, *Military History of Mississippi: 1803–1898* (Spartanburg, S.C.: Reprint Company, 1978), 74; *Record of Confederate Soldiers, War 1861–65*, pp. 19, 24, located in the Claiborne County Courthouse, Port Gibson, Mississippi; Military Search of Samuel Ullman, Military Service Branch (NNMS), National Archives and Records Administration, Washington, D.C.

15. Rowland, *Military History of Mississippi*, 75; Military Search.

16. Interview with Newfield, 7 January 1991.

17. Rowland, *Military History of Mississippi; Record of Confederate Soldiers*, 19; James M. McPherson, *Battle Cry of Freedom: The Civil War Era* (New York: Oxford University Press, 1988), 460–71; Ullman to Fries.

18. McPherson, *Battle Cry of Freedom*, 526–45; Richard B. Morris and Jeffrey B. Morris, eds., *Encyclopedia of American History* (New York: Harper and Row, 1982), 281-83.

19. Ullman to Fries; Rowland, *Military History of Mississippi*, 77; Cowett, *Birmingham's Rabbi*, 27; Military Search. Ullman furnished a substitute, A. Peterrowfs of Kentucky, who deserted on November 17, 1862, according to the Military Search. *Records of Confederate Soldiers, War 1861–65* erroneously marks the date of Ullman's departure as November 1863.

20. Interview with Newfield, 9 August 1989, 7 January 1991; Passport no. 46929 issued to Samuel Ullman 3 March 1908, Gaggstatter Papers, Henry D. Gaggstatter Private Collection, Miami, Florida (hereinafter Gaggstatter Papers).

21. Turitz and Turitz, *Jews in Early Mississippi*, xvi; Evans, *The Provincials*, 62, 68.

3. *I Am Hebrew*

1. Ullman to Fries; [Clara Moses], *Aunt Sister's Book* (New York: n.p., 1929), 15–16, MUN Papers. Ullman wrote a letter to "My Dear Clara" dated 20 February 1923 (in Ullman's eighty-third year) in

which he described his wife's family and particularly his mother-in-law, Jannette Mayer. This letter is part of *Aunt Sister's Book*; R. Ernest Dupuy and Trevor N. Dupuy, *The Encyclopedia of Military History from 3500 B.C. to the Present* (New York: Harper and Row, 1970), 883; Harnett T. Kane, *Natchez on the Mississippi* (New York: William Morrow and Company, 1947), 18; *Biographical and Historical Memoirs of Mississippi*, 2 vols. (Chicago: The Goodspeed Publishing Company, 1891), 1: 173.

2. Ullman to Fries; *Aunt Sister's Book.*

3. Eugene B. Borowitz, *Reform Judaism Today,* Book 1, *Reform in the Process of Change* (New York: Behrman House, 1978), 3, 12–13; Roy A. Rosenberg, *The Concise Guide to Judaism History, Practice, and Faith* (New York: NAL Books, 1990), 135–36; Joseph L. Blau, ed., *Reform Judaism: A Historical Perspective* (New York: KTAV Publishing House, 1973), 1, 27, 47, 105; Evans, *The Provincials,* 46–48.

4. Ullman to Fries; lecture by Samuel Ullman delivered Yom Kippur, 1876, Natchez, Mississippi, MUN Papers. Copy in possession of author. For a discussion of the Pittsburgh Platform see Cowett, *Birmingham's Rabbi,* 62.

5. Ullman to Fries; *Aunt Sister's Book,* 16; Turitz and Turitz, *Jews in Early Mississippi,* xii; [Rabbi Julius Kernan], "The Story of Temple B'nai Israel," reproduced in the *Natchez* (Miss.) *Democrat,* 18 September 1975. No copies of the original work were located and this is the only form the author could locate.

6. Turitz and Turitz, *Jews in Early Mississippi,* 14, 20; Newfield Bible; document copied by Hattie Beekman Laub from old minute book, p. 1, November 1936, located in the files of Temple B'nai Israel, Natchez, Mississippi (hereinafter Temple B'nai Israel Records); "The Story of Temple B'nai Israel," 11 September 1975.

7. Jannette Mayer to Mr. and Mrs. Dahlsheimer, 22 May 1867, Newfield Papers.

8. "Married," Natchez *Tri-Weekly Democrat,* 28 September 1867.

9. *Aunt Sister's Book,* 18.

10. *Complete Directory of the City of Vicksburg and Business Directories of Yazoo City, Jackson and Natchez,* 1877, pp. 235–39, located in Historic Natchez Association office, Natchez, Mississippi; *Natchez Directory,* 1877–78, pp. 236–37, located in Historic Natchez Association

office; Turitz and Turitz, *Jews in Early Mississippi*, 20; Jacob Ullman notes in Lehman papers.

11. R. G. Dun Records, January 1867–July 1879 (Boston: Harvard Business School, Baker Library, Manuscripts Department), 116, 123, 131.

12. *Natchez Weekly Democrat*, 22 November 1871, 18 September 1872.

13. Newfield Bible. Henry died at twenty-eight days of age and Elenora died only two days after birth.

14. "The Story of Temple B'nai Israel," 18 September 1975; document in minute book, Temple B'nai Israel Records.

15. Mrs. Henry (Melanie M.) Frank, *A Reminiscent View: 50 Years History of Ladies Aid Society of Temple B'nai Israel* (handwritten copy found in Temple B'nai Israel Records, dated 26 April 1916).

16. "Story of Temple B'nai Israel."

17. Handwritten memo regarding trouble within congregation B'nai Israel, Newfield Papers; "Story of Temple B'nai Israel," 25 September 1975; Invitation to Dedication Ceremonies of Our Temple, "Hebra Kedusha" Congregation, Natchez, Mississippi, 8 March 1872, undated, untitled scrapbook, Temple B'nai Israel Records; invitation to Grand Masquerade and Fancy Dress Ball, 7 March 1872, undated, untitled scrapbook, Temple B'nai Israel Records; "Temple in Natchez dedicated," *Natchez Tri-Weekly Democrat*, 8 March 1872, Newfield Papers.

18. Samuel Ullman to Solomon Marx, 8 June 1875, 23 September 1878, MUN Papers; lecture by Samuel Ullman, Rosh Hashanah 1877, Natchez, Mississippi, MUN Papers. Copies in possession of author. In his 8 June 1875 letter to Solomon Marx, Ullman wrote that he was filling in as rabbi for a Dr. Norden. In his letter to Clara in *Aunt Sister's Book*, he mentions a Dr. David Sterne whose position he may have filled on the latter occasion. Records for Temple B'nai Israel are sparse and mention no rabbis during the period to which Ullman refers.

19. Undated, untitled document on history of B'nai Israel congregation in Lehman Papers; Ben Isaacson and Deborah Wigoder, *The International Jewish Encyclopedia* (Englewood Cliffs: Prentice Hall, 1973), 56; B'nai B'rith record book, Ezra Lodge no. 134, IOBB,

pp. 32, 38, Temple B'nai Israel Records; Interview with Newfield, 13 November 1989.

20. Natchez, "Minutes of Mayor and Aldermen, 4 January, 1872–30 June 1879," 547, 557–58, 637, 645–46, 738, located in mayor's office, City Hall, Natchez, Mississippi; "Official Directory for 1876," *Natchez Daily Democrat*, 7 October 1876; *Complete Directory of Vicksburg*, 218; *Natchez City Directory 1877–78*, 218; Natchez, "Minutes of Mayor and Aldermen, 1879–1882," 2; Ullman to Marx, 23 September 1878.

21. Natchez, "Minutes of Mayor and Aldermen, 1879–1882," 57, 67.

22. Natchez, minutes of school board, 1880–1905 (unpaginated, dated, located in Library-Media Services, Natchez-Adams School District, Natchez, Mississippi), 15 October 1880, 27 September 1881, 3 November 1882, 17 September 1883.

23. Ibid., 7 October 1881, 21 October 1881, 21 September 1882, 31 October 1882.

24. Ibid., 27 October 1882, 31 October 1882, 9 June 1882.

25. "Tribute to our efficient trustee," resolution of teachers and principal of Natchez Union School, 21 April 1884, located in MUN Papers. Copy in possession of author.

26. Program, dedicatory services of second Temple B'nai Israel, 1905, scrapbook, Temple B'nai Israel Records; Newfield Bible.

4. The Birmingham Years: Educator

1. Edward S. LaMonte, *George B. Ward: Birmingham's Urban Statesman* (Birmingham: Oxmoor Press, 1974), 14; Martha Mitchell Bigelow, "Birmingham: Biography of a City of the New South." (Ph.D. diss., University of Chicago, 1946), 31, 63–100.

2. Ethel Armes, *The Story of Coal and Iron in Alabama* (Birmingham: Bookkeepers Press, 1972), 344; C. Vann Woodward, *Origins of the New South* (Baton Rouge: Louisiana State University Press, 1951), 127, 136.

3. Bigelow, "Birmingham," 56–57, 63–67, 194; Malcolm C. McMillan, *Yesterday's Birmingham* (Miami, Fla.: E. A. Seemann Publishing, 1975), 38; *Birmingham City Directory, 1884*, p. 155.

4. *Birmingham City Directory*, *1884*, p. 155; *1886*, p. 174; *1888*, pp. 47, 339, 512; *1890*, pp. 22, 483; *Birmingham Suburban and Bessemer Directory*, *1888–89*, p. 47; letterhead of Ullman Hardware, 19th Street and 3rd Avenue, 24 October 1887, located in Newfield Papers; Robert G. Corley, *Paying "Civic Rent": The Jews of Emanu-El and the Birmingham Community* (Birmingham: A. H. Cather Publishing Company, 1982), n.p.; Carl V. Harris, *Political Power in Birmingham 1871–1921* (Knoxville: University of Tennessee Press, 1977), 23. William Handy, J. D. S. Davis, David Ingram Purser, and Eugene F. Enslen were also officers in the Lakeside Land Company, which had an initial capitalization of $5,000 not to exceed $300,000. Established to buy, sell, and lease property, Lakeside Land Company had disappeared from city records by 1890. Jefferson County [Alabama] Probate Records, 1887, Book A, p. 8. Also in Newfield Papers.

5. John Newfield to Mayer Newfield, 23 July 1988, MUN Papers; Harris, *Political Power in Birmingham*, 55; Virginia V. Hamilton, *Alabama: A Bicentennial History* (New York: W. W. Norton and Company, 1977), 143; Rose McDavid Munger, comp., *Pioneer Scrapbook* (Birmingham: Birmingham Publishing Company, 1967), does not list Ullman among members of the "first" social clubs in the city in the 1890s.

6. Phillips was superintendent of the Birmingham school system for thirty-eight years. Bigelow, "Birmingham," 219, 227; McMillan, *Yesterday's Birmingham*; LaMonte, *George B. Ward*, 28; L. Fraser Banks, superintendent of Birmingham schools, to Bernard Postal, Director of Public Information, National Jewish Welfare Board, New York, 4 March 1955, MUN Papers; Birmingham Board of Education, minute book, 1884–1904; Charles Wilson Dabney, *Universal Education in the South* (Chapel Hill: University of North Carolina Press, 1936), 402.

7. Birmingham Board of Education, minute book, 11 August 1884, 29 August 1884, 2 September 1884.

8. Ibid., 28 October 1884, 17 April 1888, 7 September 1888.

9. Ibid., 3 March 1885.

10. Ibid., 12 October 1886, 14 December 1886, 5 April 1887, 1 December 1885.

11. Ibid., 20 November 1888, 30 July 1889, 1 and 3 August 1889; "Don't Like Order," *Birmingham News*, 23 November 1888. No

explanation was offered for parental resistance to moving the German language classes to the high school level. Perhaps fewer students pursued education into the higher level, or there may have been a belief that the language was learned more easily at an earlier age.

12. Birmingham Board of Education, minute book, 5 January 1889, 8 February 1889, 5 March 1889, 3 April 1889, 5 November 1889.

13. Ibid., 3 February 1891, 3 March 1891, 13 September 1892.

14. Ibid., 3 January 1893, 14 June 1893, 19 July 1893, 2 April 1894.

15. Ibid., 4 September 1894, 15 December 1894, January 1897–May 1898 inclusive, 6 February 1899, 15 May 1899, 2 October 1899.

16. Ibid., 12 September 1893, 5 December 1893. The breakdown of the student population given by Phillips was: 1883 white student population, 955; black student population, 560; 1893 white student population, 4,832; black student population, 5,292.

17. Dewey W. Grantham, *Southern Progressivism: The Reconciliation of Progress and Tradition* (Knoxville: University of Tennessee Press, 1983), 246–47; James D. Anderson, *The Education of Blacks in the South: 1860–1935* (Chapel Hill: University of North Carolina Press, 1988). 80–82.

18. *Montgomery Advertiser,* quoted in Horace Mann Bond, *Negro Education in Alabama: A Study in Cotton and Steel* (New York: Atheneum, 1969), 230.

19. Anderson, *Education of Blacks,* 100; Carl V. Harris, "Stability and Change in Discrimination against Black Public Schools: Birmingham, 1871–1931," *Journal of Southern History* 51 (August 1985): 403–6; Bigelow, "Birmingham," 229.

20. Birmingham Board of Education, minute book, 17 October 1885; *A Century of Reverence 1882–1982: Temple Emanu-El Centennial* (Birmingham: Temple Emanu-El, 1982), 31, located in Tutwiler Collection of Southern History and Literature, Birmingham Public Library (hereinafter Tutwiler Collection); Report of Committee on Instruction, *Annual Report of the Birmingham Schools for 1887* (Birmingham: Herald Book and Job Rooms, 1887), 15; idem, *Annual Report of the Birmingham Schools for 1891* (Birmingham: Herald Book and Job Rooms, 1891), 17, Tutwiler Collection.

21. Birmingham Board of Education, minute book, 2 March 1896; *Century of Reverence*, 31; Report of Committee on Instruction, *Annual Report of the Birmingham Public Schools for 1899* (Birmingham: Herald Book and Job Rooms, 1899), 12; Corley, *Paying "Civic Rent"*; Harris, *Political Power in Birmingham*, 173.

22. Arthur Harold Parker, *A Dream That Came True: Autobiography of A. H. Parker* (n.p., n.d.), 34, Tutwiler Collection; Harris, "Stability and Change," 403; Anderson, *Education of Blacks*, 196–97; Birmingham Board of Education, minute book, 7 May 1900, 9 June 1900.

23. Anderson, *Education of Blacks*, 196–98; Harris, "Stability and Change"; Parker, *Dream That Came True*, 34–38; Corley, *Paying "Civic Rent"*; Dabney, *Universal Education*, 406; Harris, "Stability and Change"; Anderson, *Education of Blacks*, 198.

24. Charles E. Wynes, ed., *Forgotten Voices: Dissenting Southerners in an Age of Conformity* (Baton Rouge: Louisiana State University Press, 1967), 3.

25. Cowett, *Birmingham's Rabbi*, 30; Corley, *Paying "Civic Rent"*; "Samuel Ullman," [Birmingham] *Age-Herald*, 20 January 1901; Birmingham Board of Education, minute book, 7 January 1901, 6 January 1902.

26. Birmingham Board of Education, minute book, 6 November 1900, 6 October 1902, 5 December 1904; Cowett, *Birmingham's Rabbi*, 29–30; LaMonte, *George Ward*, 30; Banks to Postal, 4 March 1955, Samuel Ullman Vertical File, Tutwiler Collection; undated newspaper clipping, Newfield Papers. Ullman Elementary School, located at 1212 Seventh Avenue South, was converted into a black high school in 1937 and was taken over by the University of Alabama at Birmingham in 1971. "Ullman Building to Be Historic Site," *Birmingham News*, 26 October 1980.

27. Cowett, *Birmingham's Rabbi*, 29–30.

5. The Birmingham Years: Rabbi

1. Helen Bethea, ed., *The Hillman Hospital: A Story of the Growth and Development of the First Hospital in Birmingham, 1888–1907* (n.p., April 1928), 11–13, located in Tutwiler Collection; Leah Rawls Atkins, *The Valley and the Hills: Birmingham and Jefferson County* (Woodland

Hills, Calif.: Windsor Publications, 1981), 71; Corley, *Paying "Civic Rent"*, "Death of a Noble Woman," *Birmingham State-Herald*, 5 March 1896; "Last Solemn Rites," *Birmingham State-Herald*, 7 March 1896. Temple Emanu-El minute book for 1892–1913, p. 66, indicates that bills of $10 for flowers and $67 for rental of two carriages that were used by "Rabbi" Ullman and his family were paid by the temple.

2. Ann Cottrell Free, "City humane society doing inadequate job," *Birmingham News*, 15 January 1974; Clarke Stallworth, "A Day in the Life of Alabama," *Birmingham News*, 28 August 1983; Mark H. Elovitz, *A Century of Jewish Life in Dixie: The Birmingham Experience* (University: University of Alabama Press, 1974), 17; *Century of Reverence*, 18, 30.

3. George Cruickshank, *A History of Birmingham and Its Environs*, 2 vols. (Chicago: Lewis Publishing Company, 1920) 1: 283; Elovitz, *Century of Jewish Life*, 10–18; Morris Newfield, "The History of the Jews in Birmingham," *The Reform Advocate*, 4 November 1911, 5–7, 9; *Century of Reverence*, 29.

4. President's Report, 4 September 1887, Temple Emanu-El, minute book, 1887–91, pp. 29–40.

5. Ibid., 18 March 1888, 3 June 1888, 1 August 1888, 4 April 1889, pp. 52–89.

6. Ibid., 20 and 28 April. No given names of Eisenberg's accusers appear in minute book records or newspaper accounts of the incident. However, Phillip A. Fox joined the congregation a few months before the controversy occurred, and appears to be the most likely candidate for accuser.

7. Ibid., 18 May, 29 June, 1, 2 and 7 July, 3 and 31 August, 3 and 7 September, 1890, pp. 113–29; Cowett, *Birmingham's Rabbi*, 25; M[ax] Samfield to Samuel Ullman, 21 May 1890, located in Temple Emanu-El minute book, 1887–91. Samfield asked for information about the scandal because of the numerous inquiries he had received about the matter.

8. Temple Emanu-El, minute book, 1887–91, 1 July, 31 August, 3 and 28 September 1890, pp. 121–33.

9. Samfield to Ullman, 1 June 1890; Temple Emanu-El, minute book, 1887–91, 7 December 1890, pp. 136–37.

10. Ullman message to congregation, Temple Emanu-El, minute

book, 1887–91, 3 August 1891; Ullman to Fries. Ullman accepted the call on 21 December 1890.

11. Newfield, "History of the Jews," 11; Elovitz, *Century of Jewish Life*, 17, 41; Ullman message to congregation, Temple Emanu-El, minute book, 1887–91, loose, unpaginated; Temple Emanu-El minute book, 1887–91, 26 May 1891, p. 143; Annual Report of President of Congregation, Temple Emanu-El, minute book, 1887–91, loose and undated, although clearly fall 1891.

12. Temple Emanu-El, minute book, 1892–1913, 25 June, 30 July, 2 August 1893, pp. 17–23.

13. Ibid., 11 February 1894, p. 32; Elovitz, *Century of Jewish Life*, 24–40.

6. *Living Young*

1. Oliver D. Street to S. D. Weakley, 23 January 1897, located in Street Collection, Gorgas Library, University of Alabama, Tuscaloosa, Alabama; *Birmingham City Directories, 1896–1908*. City directories continue to list Ullman as "salesman" until 1918, which may indicate that Ullman continued a part-time relationship with the company until that date.

2. Interview with Newfield, 9 August 1989; Ullman to Fries; Cowett, *Birmingham's Rabbi*, 24, 32, 51; Ullman to Leah U. Newfield, 5 April 1909, 25 and 30 July 1902, in Newfield Papers; Barbara Olson and Eric Olson, "A Tale of Youth," *Birmingham Magazine* 28 (July 1988): 46.

3. Samuel Ullman to Leah U. Newfield, 18 July 1902, in MUN Papers. Copy in possession of author.

4. Samuel Ullman to Leah U. Newfield, 6 July, 18 July 1902, August 1902 (no day given), in MUN Papers. Copies in possession of author.

5. Elaine U. Lehman, letter to author, 25 January 1990; interview with Newfield, 9 August 1989; bulletin, dedication of Temple Emanu-El, Birmingham, Alabama, 6, 7, and 8 March 1914, Newfield Papers.

6. Unpublished and undated letter from Samuel Ullman to

editor, Birmingham *Age-Herald* (c. 1911), Gaggstatter Papers, copy in possession of author; see also Wayne Flynt, *Poor but Proud* (Tuscaloosa: University of Alabama Press, 1989), 243–77.

7. Unpublished letter from Samuel Ullman to editor, Birmingham *Age-Herald*, Gaggstatter Papers, copy in possession of author. Though undated, the letter mentions the upcoming election of 29 November 1909.

8. Interview with Newfield, 9 August 1989. "The Passing" was written on 14 November 1920 in memory of Block, who died on 9 November 1920.

9. Quoted in Elovitz, *Century of Jewish Life*, 31; John Herbert Phillips to Samuel Ullman, 12 April 1920, MUN Papers.

10. Ullman's grandson Mayer U. Newfield was quoted in Olson and Olson, "A Tale of Youth," 46, as saying, "I never recall a pessimistic remark from him."

Bibliography

Books, Articles, and Manuscript Collections

Anderson, James D. *The Education of Blacks in the South: 1860–1935.* Chapel Hill: University of North Carolina Press, 1988.

Armes, Ethel. *The Story of Coal and Iron in Alabama.* Birmingham: Bookkeepers Press, 1972.

"As Young as your Faith." *Time.* 65 (7 February 1955): 14.

Atkins, Leah Rawls. *The Valley and the Hills: Birmingham and Jefferson County.* Woodland Hills, Calif.: Windsor Publications, 1981.

Bethea, Helen, ed. *The Hillman Hospital: A Story of the Growth and Development of the First Hospital in Birmingham, 1888–1907.* April 1928. Located in the Tutwiler Collection of Southern History and Literature, Birmingham Public Library, Birmingham, Alabama.

Bigelow, Martha Mitchell. "Birmingham: Biography of a City of the New South." Ph.D. diss., University of Chicago, 1946.

Biographical and Historical Memoirs of Mississippi. 2 vols. Chicago: Goodspeed Publishing Company, 1891.

Birmingham *Age-Herald.* 1901.

Birmingham, Alabama, city directories. 1884–1924. Located in the Tutwiler Collection of Southern History and Literature, Birmingham Public Library, Birmingham, Alabama.

Birmingham Board of Education. Minute books, 1884–1904. Department of Archives and Manuscripts, Birmingham Public Library, Birmingham, Alabama.

Birmingham News. 1888, 1964, 1974, 1980, 1983, 1987, 1988.

Birmingham State-Herald. 1896.

Blau, Joseph L., ed. *Reform Judaism: A Historical Perspective.* New York: KTAV Publishing House, 1973.

Bond, Horace Mann. *Negro Education in Alabama: A Study in Cotton and Steel.* New York: Atheneum, 1969.

Borowitz, Eugene B. *Reform Judaism Today.* Book 1, *Reform in the Process of Change.* New York: Behrman House, 1978.

A Century of Reverence 1882–1982: Temple Emanu-El Centennial. Birmingham: Temple Emanu-El, 1982. Located in the Tutwiler Collection of Southern History and Literature, Birmingham Public Library, Birmingham, Alabama.

Claiborne County, Mississippi. Record of Confederate soldiers, War of 1861–65. Located in Claiborne County Courthouse, Port Gibson, Mississippi.

Cohen, Joseph. "Early Louisville Jewish History." *The Chronicler* 8 (1920): 3–5.

Corley, Robert G. *Paying "Civic Rent": The Jews of Emanu-El and the Birmingham Community.* Birmingham: A. H. Cather Publishing Company, 1982.

Cowett, Mark. *Birmingham's Rabbi: Morris Newfield and Alabama, 1895–1940.* Tuscaloosa: University of Alabama Press, 1986.

Cruickshank, George. *A History of Birmingham and Its Environs.* 2 vols. Chicago: Lewis Publishing Company, 1920.

Dabney, Charles William. *Universal Education in the South.* Chapel Hill: University of North Carolina Press, 1936.

Dupuy, R. Ernest, and Trevor N. Dupuy. *The Encyclopedia of Military History from 3500 B.C. to the Present.* New York: Harper and Row, 1970.

Elovitz, Mark H. *A Century of Jewish Life in Dixie: The Birmingham Experience.* University: University of Alabama Press, 1974.

Evans, Eli. *The Provincials: A Personal History of Jews in the South.* New York: Atheneum, 1973.

Flynt, Wayne. *Poor but Proud: Alabama's Poor Whites.* Tuscaloosa: University of Alabama Press, 1989.

Gaggstatter, Henry D. Private collection. Miami, Florida.

Grantham, Dewey W. *Southern Progressivism: The Reconciliation of Progress and Tradition.* Knoxville: University of Tennessee Press, 1983.

Greaves, Richard L., Robert Zoller, Philip V. Cannistraro, and Rhoads Murphy. *Civilizations of the World.* New York: Harper and Row Publishers, 1990.

Hamilton, Virginia Van der Veer. *Alabama: A Bicentennial History.* New York: W. W. Norton and Company, 1977.

Harris, Carl V. *Political Power in Birmingham: 1871–1921.* Knoxville, University of Tennessee Press, 1977.

————. "Stability and Change in Discrimination against Black Public Schools: Birmingham, 1871–1931." *Journal of Southern History* 51 (1985): 375–416.

Headley, Katy McCaleb. *Claiborne County, Mississippi: The Promised Land.* Port Gibson, Miss.: Claiborne County Historical Society, 1976. Located at Port Gibson City Hall.

A History of the Jews of Louisville, Ky. Illustrated with Magnificent Half-Tone Cuts of Prominent Jews, Jewesses, Clubs, Temples, etc. New Orleans: Jewish Historical History [Louisiana], c. 1900.

"How to Stay Young." *Reader's Digest.* December 1945.

"How to Stay Young." *This Week.* 30 September 1945.

Isaacson, Ben, and Deborah Wigoder. *The International Jewish Encyclopedia.* Englewood Cliffs: Prentice Hall, 1973.

James, D. Clayton. *Antebellum Natchez.* Baton Rouge: Louisiana State University Press, 1968.

————. *The Years of MacArthur.* Vol. 3, *Triumph and Disaster, 1945–1964.* Boston: Houghton-Mifflin Company, 1985.

"Japan." *Forbes* 144 (24 July 1989): 176.

Jefferson County, Alabama, probate records. Book A, 1887. Located in Jefferson County Courthouse, Birmingham, Alabama.

Johnston, J. Stoddard, ed. *Memorial History of Louisville from Its First Settlement to the Year 1896.* 2 vols. Chicago and New York: American Biographical Publishing Company, 1896.

Kane, Harnett T. *Natchez on the Mississippi.* New York: William Morrow and Company, 1947.

Kennedy, Edward M. "A Tribute to His Brother." *Vital Speeches of the Day* 34 (1 July 1968): 546–47.

[Kernan, Rabbi Julius]. "The Story of Temple B'nai Israel." Serialized and reproduced in *Natchez* (Miss.) *Democrat,* 11, 18, 25 September and 2 October 1975.

LaMonte, Edward S. *George B. Ward: Birmingham's Urban Statesman.* Birmingham: Oxmoor Press, 1974.

Landau, Herman. *Adath Louisville: The Story of a Jewish Community.* Louisville, Ky.: Herman Landau and Associates, 1981.

Langer, William L., comp. and ed. *An Encyclopedia of World History.* Boston: Houghton Mifflin Company, 1972.

Lehman, Mrs. Robert (Elaine). Private collection. Natchez, Mississippi.

Louisville, Kentucky, city directory. 1861. Located in the University of Louisville Department of Archives and Records, Louisville, Kentucky.

MacArthur, General Douglas. Papers. MacArthur Memorial, Norfolk, Virginia.

McLemore, Richard Aubrey, ed. *A History of Mississippi.* 2 vols. Hattiesburg: University and College Press of Mississippi, 1973.

McMillan, Malcolm C. *Yesterday's Birmingham.* Miami: E. A. Seemann Publishing, 1975.

McPherson, James M. *Battle Cry of Freedom: The Civil War Era.* New York: Oxford University Press, 1988.

Military Service Branch, National Archives and Records Administration, Washington, D.C. Veterans Records. Military search, Samuel Ullman. Company G, Sixteenth Mississippi Infantry.

Miyazawa, Jiro. *Youth.* Privately published, n.d.

Morris, Richard B., and Jeffrey B. Morris, eds. *Encyclopedia of American History.* New York: Harper and Row, 1982.

[Moses, Clara.] *Aunt Sister's Book.* New York: Privately published, 1929. In possession of Mayer U. Newfield.

Munger, Rose McDavid, comp. *Pioneer Scrapbook.* Birmingham: Birmingham Publishing Company, 1967.

Natchez Daily Democrat. 1876.

Natchez, Mississippi, city directories. 1877–78. Located in Historic Natchez Association office, Natchez, Mississippi.

Natchez (Mississippi) Democrat. 1975.

Natchez, Mississippi. Minutes of mayor and aldermen, 1872–1882. Office of the Mayor, City Hall.

Natchez, Mississippi. Minutes of school board, 1880–1905. Library-Media Services, Natchez-Adams School District.

Natchez *Tri-Weekly Democrat.* 1867, 1872.

Natchez Weekly Democrat. 1871–1872.

Newfield family Bible. In possession of Mrs. Semon Ullman Newfield. Birmingham, Alabama.

Newfield, Mayer Ullman. Private collection. Birmingham, Alabama.

Newfield, Morris. "The History of the Jews in Birmingham." *The Reform Advocate*. 4 November 1911: 6–33.

————. Papers. Department of Archives and Manuscripts, Birmingham Public Library, Birmingham, Alabama.

New York Times. 1989.

"Notes and Comments." *New Yorker* 30 (5 February 1955): 21–22.

Olson, Barbara, and Eric Olson. "A Tale of Youth." *Birmingham Magazine*. 28 (1988): 44–47.

Parker, Arthur Harold. *A Dream That Came True: Autobiography of A. H. Parker*. Tutwiler Collection of Southern History and Literature, Birmingham Public Library, Birmingham, Alabama.

Pittsburgh Press. 1 July 1990.

Report of the Committee on Instruction. *Annual Report of the Birmingham Public Schools for 1887*. Tutwiler Collection of Southern History and Literature, Birmingham Public Library, Birmingham, Alabama.

R. G. Dun Records. January 1867–July 1879. Baker Library, Harvard Business School, Boston, Massachusetts.

Rosenberg, Roy A. *The Concise Guide to Judaism History, Practice and Faith*. New York: NAL Books, 1990.

Rowland, Dunbar. *Military History of Mississippi: 1803–1898*. Spartanburg, S.C.: Reprint Company, 1978.

Sachar, Abram Leon. *A History of the Jews*. New York: Alfred A. Knopf, 1965.

Sokolsky, George E. "From a Summit of Years — Four Score." New York *Journal American*, 10 March 1955.

Street, Oliver D. Street Collection. Gorgas Library, University of Alabama, Tuscaloosa, Alabama.

Temple B'nai Israel. Records. Natchez, Mississippi.

Temple Emanu-El. Minute books, 1887–1913. Department of Archives and Manuscripts, Birmingham Public Library, Birmingham, Alabama.

Temple Gemiluth Chassed. 1859 cash book. Located in American Jewish Archives, Hebrew Union College, Cincinnati, Ohio.

"The General's Moment." *Newsweek* 45 (17 February 1955): 22.

Turitz, Leo E., and Evelyn Turitz. *Jews in Early Mississippi.* Jackson: University Press of Mississippi, 1983.

Ullman, Samuel. Vertical file. Tutwiler Collection of Southern History and Literature, Birmingham Public Library, Birmingham, Alabama.

Vicksburg, Mississippi, city directory. 1877. Located in Historic Natchez Association office, Natchez, Mississippi.

Warren, Harris Gaylord. "People and Occupations in Port Gibson, 1860." *Journal of Mississippi History* 10 (April 1948): 104–15.

Woodward, C. Vann. *Origins of the New South.* Baton Rouge: Louisiana State University Press, 1951.

Wynes, Charles E., ed. *Forgotten Voices: Dissenting Southerners in an Age of Conformity.* Baton Rouge: Louisiana State University Press, 1967.

Interviews

Boone, Edward J., Jr. Archivist, MacArthur Memorial, Norfolk, Virginia. Telephone interview, 10 January 1990.

Newfield, Mayer U. Birmingham, Alabama. 9 August 1989, 13 November 1989, 7 January 1991.

Personal Correspondence

Edward Forman, NBC News "Sunday Today," to author, 23 December 1991.

Tatsuro Ishida to author, 8 March 1990.

Elaine Lehman to author, 25 January 1990.

Jiro Miyazawa to author, 1 June 1992.

Munehisa Sakuyama to author, 23 February 1990.

Osamu Uno to author, 23 February 1990.

Video

"A Bridge Called 'The Youth.'" 1987. English version in author's possession and in Mayer U. Newfield collection.

1875, 1878   Letters. Ullman to Solomon Marx. Mayer U. Newfield Papers, Birmingham, Alabama.

1876   Lecture, Yom Kippur. Mayer U. Newfield Papers, Birmingham, Alabama.

1877   Lecture, Rosh Hashanah. Mayer U. Newfield Papers, Birmingham, Alabama.

1887   President's report. Temple Emanu-El minute book. Department of Archives and Manuscripts, Birmingham Public Library, Birmingham, Alabama.

1891   Messages. Temple Emanu-El minute book. Department of Archives and Manuscripts, Birmingham Public Library, Birmingham, Alabama.

1902, 1909   Letters. Samuel Ullman to Leah U. Newfield. Morris Newfield Papers, Department of Archives and Manuscripts, Birmingham Public Library, Birmingham, Alabama.

1901–1911 (?)   Unpublished letters to editor, Birmingham *Age-Herald*, regarding prohibition and mining legislation. Henry D. Gaggstatter Papers, Miami, Florida.

1915   Untitled poem on grandson, Lincoln Newfield, seeking warmth from rock. Mayer U. Newfield Papers, Birmingham, Alabama.

17 July 1920   Letter to Richard Fries. Morris Newfield Papers. Department of Archives and Manuscripts, Birmingham Public Library, Birmingham, Alabama.

1920   "The Passing." Poem written at the death of nephew, Laurens Block. Mayer U. Newfield Papers, Birmingham, Alabama.

1922   *From the Summit of Years, Four Score.* Los Angeles: Fred S. Lang Company Publishers. In author's possession and Mayer U. Newfield Papers, Birmingham, Alabama.

1922   "Why Tears?" Poem written in Dallas, Texas, when

Ullman was 82 years of age. Mayer U. Newfield Papers, Birmingham, Alabama.

1929   "John Mayer and His Wife." In [Clara Moses], *Aunt Sister's Book*, 15–19. New York: Privately published, 1929. Mayer U. Newfield Papers, Birmingham, Alabama.

Index

Ullman, Samuel, poems of, 67–124; "All is Benign," 76; "By Their Hands Will You Know Them," 83; "Cupid," 84; "Day," 108; "Death," 97; "Design or Fate?," 71; "A Dream," 109; "A Dream and Its Message," 91; "Dust to Dust," 98; "Duty," 116; "Echoes," 106; "Goals," 99; "Growing Apace," 117; "I Am Merry When I May," 123; "An Invocation," 92; "Israel — The Dreamer," 73; "It Matters Not," 117; "Justice–," 77; "Justice and Love," 78; "A Lay of Cheer," 122; "Love–," 78; "March Fourth," 86; "Mars and Mammon," 72; "The Master Weaver," 107; "Meditation," 97; "Midnight Musings," 92; "Musings," 87; "My Pipe," 116; "Mysteries," 105; "Night," 108; "On Seeing a Skeleton (In a Dream)," 99; "Our Betrothal," 85; "The Passing," 63, 101; "Patience and Will," 107; "Smile," 120; "A Song of Praise and Faith," 110; "The Speed Demon," 98; "Tell Me," 121; "Thy Trace," 71; "Time," 105; "To the Memory of Her Who Was of Me a Part," 85; "Tomorrow," 87; "A Tried Remedy," 119; "Untitled," 115; "Valentines on Life's Highways," 118; "A Vision and a Hope," 78; "Visions," 79; "Weaving," 118; "What of Tomorrow?," 75; "What's Your Hurry?," 61, 113; "Why Tears?," 100; "Yesterday and Today," 88; "You and I," 116; "Youth," v, ix, x, 1, 3–10, 62, 113

Ullman, Samuel (relative in Louisville), 14

Ullman, Rabbi Samuel ben Isaac (grandfather), 11

Ullman, Sidney Mayer (son), 25

Ullman, Simon (cousin), 13

Ullman and Company (Louisville), 14

Ullman and Laub Mercantile (Natchez), 22–24

Ullman Building (Birmingham), 44–45

Ullman Clothing Store (Natchez), 58

Ullman Hardware Company (Birmingham), 32

Ullman School (Birmingham), 43–44

Union School (Natchez), 29–30

University of Alabama at Birmingham, The, x, xi, 7, 9, 44–45; Medical Center, 48

Uno, Osamo, 6–9. *See also* Toyo Boseki

Valley Campaign, 17

Wall Street Journal, The, 6

Washington, George, 1

West End School, 34–35

Williams, Mary Alice, 5. *See also* NBC "Sunday Today"

Woodward, C. Vann, 31

Wordsworth, William, 5

"Youth" (poem). *See* Ullman,
   Samuel, poems of
Youth Association, The
   (Japan), x, 8